The Gift of Spirit

. . . .

Creating a Pathway to Healing,
Harmony, and Sacred Balance

TINA COLUCCIO

TURNING
STONE
PRESS

First published in 2012 by
Turning Stone Press, an imprint of
Red Wheel/Weiser, LLC
With offices at:
665 Third Street, Suite 400
San Francisco, CA 94107
www.redwheelweiser.com

ISBN: 978-1-61852-010-4 (ppb)
ISBN: 978-1-61852-009-8 (hardcover)

Library of Congress Cataloging-in-Publication Data
available upon request

Cover design by Jim Warner
Cover photograph ©
Interior design by Patrick Cunningham

Printed in the United States of America
IBT
10 9 8 7 6 5 4 3 2 1

☞ Contents ☜

*To my daughter—Taylor Malani—my Hawaiian
princess, who broke through to this earth-plane and
demanded my spiritual awakening. Through your birth
came the birth of my awareness and the true beginning
of my spiritual journey. You were a vehicle of great
knowledge and of great power.*

*To my son—Frank Steven—I connected to your soul in
heavenly realms, calling me. You were waiting, and you
were welcomed here with arms wide open. I see in your
eyes, so serendipitously blue, an ocean of dreams waiting for you to sail into. Your greatness is amazing.*

*To my son—Steven Joseph—you descended from the
heavens above as my angel to love and heal my broken
heart and wipe the tears from my eyes. The gentleness
of your hand wrapped around my heart will remain
imprinted until the end of time. You are, and forever
will be, my angel baby.*

Acknowledgments

I wish with all my heart and being to express my profound gratitude and graciousness to God. I would like to acknowledge my father, brothers, and mother—my family in heaven—for your presence and, most of all, your love. You became Spirit, becoming my spiritual family. You have given me the inspiration, strength, and wisdom to give others inspiration, strength, and wisdom.

I am especially grateful to my editor, Willy Mathes, whose editing talent, passion, and hope have strengthened my heart and my voice.

Introduction

There is a universal level that transcends cultural differences, like a universal gateway where all religions meet: Christianity, Judaism, Hinduism, Buddhism, etc. I call that sense of universal oneness "Spirit."

I am not sure why, perhaps because of what went on in my childhood, but I have been given the Gift of Spirit. I honor and cherish this gift, and it is my privilege to share it with you. I do so because we are of one human family, joined together by and in Spirit.

My father and my brothers passed away when I was young, and my mother passed in 2006. But they all come back to me in Spirit. They guide me and support me. They are what I call my "spirit guides."

Spirit comes to me unveiling the will of God, unveiling my own inner wisdom, and unwrapping my deepest core of intuition. When I speak throughout this book using the word "Spirit," I am speaking of Spirit as angels, God, the Universe, and spirit guides. They all derive from the same Divine Source.

This is my truth. Each one of us has our own truth, and each one of us can rely on our own intuition, our own "inner knowing," and our own spirit guides. And each one of us has God within us and God, Spirit, and angels around us and available to us at all times.

I wrote *The Gift of Spirit* to awaken the spiritual gifts inside of you. Through my own life, through my struggle, much spiritual guidance and many spiritual messages have come forward; and now I offer *The Gift of Spirit* to comfort you, to guide you, to inspire you, and to provide you with strength and confidence. We have the power to work with our destiny, with our own fate. We have the power to live in the highest possible realm on this earth and manifest our heart's truest desires.

In this book, there is spiritual, emotional, and physical healing in the offing. You may use this book in accordance with your own intuition to find this healing. Whether you soak it all in from cover to cover or randomly open it to find your guidance for the day, the answer—the guidance—is there for you.

I offer you these guiding messages from Spirit to help you find your own inner truth. I offer to you the light I have found upon my own path and the energy of love and grace to restore wholeness, oneness, and enlightenment to you. As I have heard the voice of my intuition and spirit guides, I have written them here as an offering to your highest good. These words are written through me; I am but the vessel, and I am honored, blessed, and awed at these revelations I bring to you.

Prologue

That Wednesday afternoon—late September, 2006, in the cemetery—was unlike any other in my thirty-five years of existence. The sorrow that I felt . . . I didn't know how I would feel after my mother had passed. I had thought about it but, of course, no one ever really knows what it will be like until it actually happens.

I had less guilt than I thought I would have. It had been only a few weeks as I began to write this, so I was still very much in the mourning stage . . . but I was tremendously sad. I felt so alone. Burying her was like burying my father and my two brothers all over again.

It was like a scene right out of the movies. Sitting there at the burial, in front of her casket over the vault in the ground. I couldn't help but take it all in, way deep into my heart. It was like no one else was even there. I just absorbed this . . . this feeling of completion, like this was the final death, and all of these deaths were, somehow, beyond my ability to comprehend; that they were the instruments of my progress, of my transformation.

There was both great pain and great movement, almost like a rite of passage and a gateway opening. They were all there in one view then: my father's grave, my brothers' graves, and my mother's casket, which would be lowering into the vault, into her grave. I thought, "Now everyone's gone. I feel abandoned all over again." My hurting was so enormous that I cried just like a little girl. I, in fact, *was* a little girl who had suddenly been abandoned by her family. A little girl in a woman's body.

Sitting there in front of her casket during the last moments of the burial, everyone formed a line. One by one, they sprinkled holy water on her casket, took a rose from atop the casket, and then offered their condolences to me as they passed.

The funeral director then started walking toward me with a crucifix in his hands. It was so surreal and it played out before me in slow motion. I saw him coming, and as he reached his hands out toward me to give me the gold crucifix, all I said in my mind was, "Oh, God, oh, God, please no, please no, please no."

And as the crucifix touched my hand, I saw it touch my mother's hand from Steven's burial; I saw it touch her hand from my father's burial; and then I saw it touch her hand from Kevin's burial, all like little flashes, like a movie. It was all in slow motion . . . and so intensely heartbreaking.

Inside my head, I heard myself calling out:

Oh God, I'm left here! I am left here! What am I going to do?

I remember sitting there at the burial, at the very end, after everyone had said goodbye and had walked away. I was still sitting in front of my mother's casket. I sat there for what seemed like hours, holding my hand over my mouth with one hand, and the crucifix and four roses I had picked off of the casket spray in the other hand. I had picked three red ones for my father and two brothers, and I had picked a beautiful white one for my mother. I stared at the bronze-colored casket that was held there above the vault in the ground.

To the left of me were the other graves, all in a row. Steven's, my mothers' parents', then my father's, and then Kevin's, in that order. As I held that moment in time, I felt completely open and raw. The wind blew so nicely, so crisply, like it was helping me fill my lungs to breathe. It felt so good, and, out of nowhere, I felt the presence of Spirit and peace. I felt true grace at that moment, and I soaked it all in . . . holding those four roses.

I shook my head and whispered aloud, "It looks like there are four of you now . . . four of you to have my back . . . the fantastic four." Then they said back to me, "We *are* the fantastic four."

Part I

Beginning to Heal—Connecting to Your Spiritual Support System

$\backsim$ 1 $\backsim$

The Gift of Grief and Loss

My "once upon a time" starts when I was almost six years old.

On March 9th, 1978, my eldest brother, Steven Joseph, age 19, died in Jacksonville, Florida, when he was hit by a car as he walked along the side of the road with my other brother, Kevin. The driver of the car was drunk and Steven died at the scene of the crash, which occurred around 2:40 a.m., officials said. After the collision, Kevin dropped to the ground, only to hold his brother, now dead, in his arms. He sat there in horror holding Steven's lifeless body on the side of the street waiting for help to arrive. Both of my elder brothers were in the Navy at the time, stationed in Jacksonville, Florida, and both were on their way back to continue their tour of duty on the USS Saratoga. I was almost six years old, living with my mother and father in St. Petersburg, Florida.

That day, two officers dressed in their spotless white uniforms came to the door with a telegram confirming Steven's death and providing details on the shipping of his remains. As those two officers silently walked away from the front porch, it was as though my mother's soul quietly left with them and spiraled through the air like a slow whirlwind. Death had come oh so early to the son to whom she had given life. The cyclical transformation of his birth and of his death left my mother silenced, stricken, and imprisoned in a shell of disbelief, agony, and grief.

Seven years later, on the early morning of January 13, 1985, my father, who had recently been ill with chronic obstructive pulmonary disease (COPD), was hospitalized. The phone had just rung, and I remember looking over to my mother, who was lying on the couch drinking her morning instant coffee that I had always made for her. When I ran over to the phone that sat on the floor beside the couch, I was hesitant about picking it up, but I did. The nurse on the other end of the line asked for my mother. I handed it to her, scrunched up my face, pursed my lips tight, and then ran really fast to the stairs. I sat on the third step of the orange-and-red-shag-carpeted stairs, preparing to listen to the conversation, bracing myself, grabbing a hold of the high-pile carpet with both hands like I was pulling someone's hair out, already knowing what was going to be said. After what seemed to be one long, hushed moment later, she hung up the phone on the cradle on the floor beside her, spilling her body and extremities limp over the side of the couch, and turned to me to say in a low tone, "Daddy died."

It was on that day that I came to know that I was without his protection. A truly sick sense of abandonment left me feeling gutless. My sadness turned into deep sorrow, burrowing its way into my soul, along with a hollowness that took the place of my young heart.

On April 27th, 1985, not even four months later, my brother, Kevin, who was 25 at the time, was living back home with my mother and me. At around 1 p.m., he called my mother to say that after work he was going out with a friend; so, not to wait for him to come home and eat dinner. I could immediately tell that my mother, who was very intuitive herself, didn't feel comfortable at all with the idea. In fact, her anxiety level grew after a few hours, and she called him back to try to talk him into coming home. My mother, being of Puerto Rican descent, could be quite overmothering; but sometimes she plainly called it out, like a psychic, very intuitive and keen. She explained to him she had made his favorite Spanish meal—*arroz con gondolas*—practically begging him to come home. But he did not.

The next morning, I had been sleeping with my mother in my father's spot, which had become a common occurrence since he had died. We were awakened by the phone ringing on the nightstand. She always slept on her stomach and squished her face down onto her favorite sack-like feather pillow that was once Steven's Navy pillow. I watched her extend her arm from that position and reach over to answer the phone. Within five seconds, a Tampa police detective on the other end of the phone casually, with what seemed to be a brazen voice, asked, "Is this Mrs. Mercedes Coluccio?"

"Yes," replied my mother.

The detective immediately responded, "I'm sorry; your son is dead."

All I saw was her dropping the phone in utter shock, her eyes welling up with tears, and the look of total catastrophic dismay behind those tears before they were allowed to be expelled from her once-beautiful brown eyes.

Kevin had gone to a bar in Tampa with a friend. He didn't want to drink and drive, so he let his friend drive his car after they'd had a few drinks. As they returned to St. Petersburg via the Gandy Bridge, just before 3 a.m., his friend lost control of the car, hitting the bridge's concrete abutment, and my brother was ejected from the car and killed. The car flipped over several times before coming to rest in a crumpled heap on the road. The police officials believe that, as Kevin was ejected, the car door flew open and then closed back on his upper body and head, killing him instantly. The accident occurred at approximately 2:40 a.m., officials said, which was coincidentally the same time of Steven's death seven years prior. Kevin left behind not only my mother and me, but also a beautiful three-year-old daughter named Jessie.

What were once my mother's beautiful personality characteristics—her entire identity—collapsed into nothingness through this grief and loss . . . a nothingness I then knew would last forever in this lifetime.

This once-upon-a-time is my life. But it is only a part of my story. My story was served up with much grief, much despair, much anguish, and much isolation. Through this, though, came to me a gift. And the gift was a connection to God, a connection to Spirit, and a connection to the presence of angels. They came to me in many different ways: in song, in visual images and "signs," and even in numbers. I could even hear their voices. Later I would come to understand that this was the development of my clairaudience.

∽

I say the following from experience, and from the depths of my heart: if you, too, are suffering (or have recently suffered) as I have, by opening your eyes during your time of grief and loss, you will soon discover your true convictions and the courage of those convictions. Surrender to this grief, and you will be given the Gift of Spirit. Accept the darkness and fear, feel it. Savor each moment of grief, depression, and despair—savor this feeling, really own it, and then let it go. Stay positive, be light, know that this is the lowest moment of low energy, and that you are worthy and whole and on your way up . . . to enlightenment.

When you're really on the bottom, nothing else can go wrong. Yes, it may feel like the worst, but somehow you're still breathing, whether you feel that's fortunate or unfortunate. Air is still filling your lungs. From every fall, you will eventually stand up, brush yourself off, and move forward toward your own place of empowerment and wholeness. Ask for strength, ask for the presence of God, and the presence of anyone who has passed away before you. They will come, I promise you. Your entire being will be held, comforted and surrounded by peace and love.

Death—whether the death of a loved one, the death of a relationship or marriage, or the death of oneself through a tragic event—can be useful to you. Don't let it *define* who you are. Let it *empower* who you are! Let it move you into greatness! Be birthed again, like a phoenix rising from the ashes. You are like me. This death is of deep transformation and attunement to the multitude of mini-lifetimes in this life.

In loving memory. May the souls of the beloved departed be lifted into a place of peace, refreshment, and light. And through the mercy of God, may they rest in peace. Amen.

⪻ 2 ⪼

The Gift of Intuition

What is intuition? Is it a simple tool of the mind? Or is there something more spiritual that provides us with the intuition we all seem to have? In the *American Heritage Dictionary*, many related meanings describe intuition. For the most part they seem to relate to the "ability to sense or know immediately *without* reasoning" or "immediate cognition *without* the use of rational processes."

Isn't it interesting that even the dictionary definitions of intuition acknowledge that there is something happening here *without* reason, *beyond* rational explanation? Indeed, all of us were born with some form of intuitive or "psychic" ability. However, intuition is *not* something that the logical mind can understand. It is much too intangible to put your finger on, yet every single one of us works with it and uses it every day. It is our sixth sense. We've all heard the aphorisms "Trust your gut," "Do what feels right," and "Do what your heart tells you" passed along from the wisest of our elders, and we've all done those things at some point. All of these phrases really mean one thing: listening to and using your intuition is *essential* for success in all that comes along in life.

~

In September, 2004, I was living on St. Augustine Beach in Florida. Both Hurricane Frances and Hurricane Jeanne had just blown through. On the very next day, I took the kids down to the shore. The newly renovated, beautiful, white-sand beach had been washed away. The sky was gray. There was a silent stillness in the strong wind that marked the aftermath of a torrential hurricane. The stillness I felt was related to being in the center of the eye of a hurricane. I felt safe, far removed from the violent winds that had so recently passed.

I spent some time down there at the shore, walking, sitting, the children playing. Then the clouds began to part, and there in the sky were three beautiful and separate rainbows. They appeared so amazing to me, looking like sacred symbols in the sky. I knew that Spirit was confirming my safety, telling me that I had made it through the storm, with my tiny yet strong arm holding up my white flag. Spirit was reassuring me that it was going to be okay now. The message for me also was that the time to move forward in my life was now. I felt blessed at that moment, with a sense of peace, safety, clarity, and comfort.

Trust in your intuition and believe in the signs that you receive—just as I did with these three rainbows—as they are blessings. Notice these blessings; the answers are all there. These signs are guidance being picked up by your intuition. The guidance is real and can be truly significant to your life.

The reality is that this life we're living here on earth is full of mini-lifetimes, and the only constant is change. Just by being open to change and letting your intuition guide you instead of abiding by social programming and fear, the struggle perpetuated by such programming and fear will dissipate into a flow of positive life events.

Connecting to your core of intuition, recognizing its messages, and learning from it takes practice. It is through practice that you will begin to recognize and understand intuitive feelings and visions, which can then allow you to construct your life according to this intuitive guidance. Acting on your intuition can be a richly rewarding experience.

Here are some ways to increase or heighten your intuitive ability:

Stay away from negative people or situations. Negative people and negative places contaminate you physically, emotionally, and spiritually.

Diet is a big factor, believe it or not. Drink enough water to stay well hydrated. Whole foods and raw fruits and vegetables are full of Nature's most vibrant and vital energy. They also contribute greatly to healing in general, and are certainly the way to go. To whatever extent possible, avoid sugars, white carbohydrates, and alcohol. Limit caffeine, as well. You will feel the difference if you follow these dietary guidelines. When the physical cells of your body feel nourished properly and are hydrated, your higher "intuitive cells" are elevated and clearer.

Exercise your whole self: mind, body and spirit. Set a priority to make time for physical exercise—running, walking, bicycling, anything that gets your heart pumping. Exercise produces and releases endorphins, which elevate your mood and increase intuitive awareness. Practice relaxation techniques, as well (for mental and spiritual exercise), such as guided imagery, meditation, and yoga.

Pay attention to signs and feelings. The content of your intuition is typically conveyed to you through those, and you'll likely begin noticing them all around you. I paid attention to the three rainbows (mentioned earlier in this chapter), as they were signs from Spirit telling me to *move forward.* I listened to my feelings and my intuition, which had turned into a strong inclination to move forward to Clearwater, Florida. I now know Spirit sent me there because my mother was going to pass, *and* I needed those couple of years to heal, forgive, and allow grace to come in and put closure on our lives together here on earth. It is as important to notice your true inner feelings as it is to recognize your intuition. There have been times in my life when I have been overwhelmed with fear, in a total disconnection from my true inner feelings. I found myself shaking my head and repeating, "I don't know. I don't know." I wanted someone's—anyone's—attention and help. I felt my heart was spilled out in all directions. But always at the bottom of my fear I saw my own open heart, and in reaching for understanding and a connection to Spirit, I was given clear intuition and an ability to deal with my feelings and emotions. Your connection to and awareness of these signs and feelings (and the "answers" to requests for guidance) will allow you a connection to clarity of purpose in your actions, and a clear way through each day of your life.

When you are reading or conversing with others, and something—whether it be a number, a book title, or a turn of phrase—triggers a reaction in you like that of a mild stun gun or evokes goose bumps, you must take this into your conscious thought and let it "sit in your stomach" a few moments (listen to it intuitively). In this way, the initial spark of intuition will be channeled through your sixth sense and down into the conscious thought to be assimilated. It's not your imagination that you're attending to; *it is your intuition.*

When we set aside the fear, doubt and rationality, our intuition is left shining and the way will become clear. You can start by simply asking for guidance. Ask for "signs from above." And then listen and become open. God and Spirit can *and will* send you signs in the physical world. All you have to do is ask, look, and listen with an open heart.

Here are a few key ways that Spirit (or the spirit of a deceased love one) can connect with you, sparking your intuitive ability:

Numbers. This may be a series of numbers or one number that feels special to you, a deceased love one's favorite number or numbers, or a random number that keeps appearing over and over. You'll often see these numbers in mundane places—on a clock or perhaps a receipt— and you may get an overwhelming feeling of emotion. It is then good to tune into your intuitive awareness. Both of my brothers loved the number 44; often, I'll feel their presence come strongly to me, and I'll turn around to that number on a billboard, or on a ticket, or on TV at that moment. Looking up to them as a toddler, I loved whatever they loved. Many of my childhood pictures show me with the number 44 ironed on my clothing. My father liked the numbers 1, 4, and 7. He would always play those numbers in combination in the lottery or in betting. I'll often feel his presence and look at the clock to see that it's 1:47 or 11:47, and I feel a big hug inside, knowing that it's him. My family's love is with me always, but it comes to me in particularly concentrated ways at times, and it is so clear I know it's them. They also come to me and show me signs, such as rainbows, anything with "three" in it—three candles, three birds, three boats—to represent the three of them.

Lights. The light in your area will suddenly change: lights might become dimmer or shine brighter, or the room will lighten or darken from the sunlight moving. A light bulb will flicker or burn out. This can signify that Spirit is near you or around you, and it is a way for Spirit to get your attention (i.e., Spirit is signaling you to use your intuition). One evening, I was sitting at dinner with my niece, Jessie. It was a few months after my mother had passed, and we were conversing about how lovely the funeral turned out and just generally talking about her. All of a sudden, the oil lamp on the table blew out, just as if someone leaned over and extinguished it with a big breath of air. We both immediately knew her spirit was with us.

Music. Spirit can communicate through music. It can be the lyrics of a new song or a deceased loved one's favorite song(s). My loved ones' spirits all communicate to me through songs that correspond through the timeframe of their lives and the timing of their deaths. The last movie Kevin took me to before his death was *Flashdance*. To this day, when I'm driving and I need him, I will feel his presence and a song will play from the movie. You know the ones: "Maniac" and "Flashdance . . . What a Feeling." My father also sends me songs that are special to our bond. Most songs from the rock group Chicago come from him. I can remember my brother Steven singing to my mother the song "*Lady*" by Kenny Rogers. And then there were what I'd come to know as the sad songs. When my mother would hear the song "Feelings" by Johnny Mathis or, heaven forbid, the military song "Taps," she would be overcome with devastation and begin to sob. Whatever way it comes, you may feel Spirit's presence through the song, sparking you to "tune in" to any guidance or reassuring messages.

Audio. You can hear Spirit. I hear my family members say different phrases to me: "I promise you, Tina, there is a pot of gold at the end of the rainbow," and "There is a light at the end of the tunnel; you'll see it one day," and "Turn around, bright eyes." They also come in my dreams and I can hear their voice speaking to me. I can hear their same voices that they had when they were here on earth.

Smells. Spirit can come through and communicate with you by sending you different scents. It can be the fragrance of a rose, the smell of certain clothing or fabric, or a hint of perfume. The other day, I was at work and really missed my mother; it was the anniversary of her passing. I opened a box of medical needles (I was working as an aesthetic nurse at the time) and it said "Mercedes Medical" on it. Although I'd done the exact same act many different times in the past, I had never noticed the label before that day. My mother's first name was Mercedes. After that, a new patient signed in, and she wore the same perfume as my mother used to wear, Elizabeth Arden Red Door. I could almost see my mother's face in this patient's face. I intuitively knew that my mother was with me that day, and it was very comforting.

Animals. Animals often carry significant signs from Spirit. They can convey important messages and feelings to you. I mention two helpful books relating to animal connections with Spirit in Chapter 13, "The Gift of Healing." Whenever I see deer, there are always three of them to represent the three men from my life who passed: my father and two brothers. Animals have been a constant source of messages, encouragement, and comfort. One day a few years ago, a massive swarm of bees flocked over my second-story window, like a storm cloud. The window was located in the creativity section of my home (per feng shui, pronounced "fung shway," which is discussed in detail in Chapter 10, "The Gift of Feng Shui"), and I intuitively knew they were trying to tell me something. Eventually, Spirit's message became clear: that no matter what circumstances come up, I need to prioritize the development of my work . . . that however grand my dream (this book), there would be a promise of fulfillment if I pursued it. The bee is a symbol of accomplishing goals (through work, as in "worker bees") that appear to be impossible, and Spirit was telling me to believe in my creative self, and even more specifically, to get organized and get going further on the development of *The Gift of Spirit.*

Spirit will provide us with the energy to focus on living in fulfillment and peace. Spirit can pervade all of our life situations, like a knight in shining armor. Spirit can open our hearts, bringing compassion, engendering lightness, and extending forgiveness. Spirit can illuminate our paths and set us onward to smooth sailing.

Diary Entry: December 14, 2006

Today would have been my brother Kevin's birthday. I came to the cemetery today to not only say "happy birthday," but also to see my mother's marker in the ground for the very first time. It really looked nice. As I approached my mother's marker, a comforting peaceful feeling came over me. It was so comfortable, I didn't want to move away from her grave.

My first words out loud were, "I'm happy . . . I'm happy for you, Mom. I know you wanted to go home." I stood there not moving anything, just breathing and connecting with her spirit. I said, more loudly, "Mom, I so don't want to leave, I don't want to leave you, Mom!"

And she said to me, "I am so proud of you, Tina, but it is time for you to do this."

I replied, "I don't want to leave."

She said to me again, "It's time, Tina."

I knew what was she was talking about: this book, my writing, my future, and my gift. It was never time . . . until *now*.

In that very moment, a breeze of wind wafted over me, the leaves fell off of the tree, and there was such a beautiful and crisp sound of leaves twirling in the air. The breeze was so strong that

---

it was practically pushing me—"Go, Tina, go, go!" I heard her say. It was almost like she was getting annoyed that I was taking so long to listen to her . . . to step away.

As I knelt down and kissed her marker, her final words were, "It's okay. You have the Fantastic Four now, remember? You can do this! It's time."

And as I walked away, I kept looking back over my shoulder, "I love you, Mom. Stay with me now."

I walked a few yards to Daddy's grave. I instantly smiled that ear-to-ear smile—the kind of smile that represents pure love and true joy. I can always tell when I smile like that, because it comes from within. I get that huge smile from him. And I am so grateful that that same smile is in my son, Frank.

"I love you, Daddy," I said.

He replied, "You deserve to be happy. You deserve all the happiness in the world; you deserve this."

I looked over to Kevin's grave and called out, "Happy birthday, Kevin!"

He said, "Tell Jessie that I love her."

I took a deep breath and started to walk away. I looked back and said to all of them, "Bye! Will you guys stay with me?"

"Yes, Tina, you know we will. Go ahead. We're right behind you."

Focus on Spirit. When you need Spirit, it will be there. By accessing and using your intuition, you can feel it, see it, hear it, and sense it. Look for anything that you might understand to be a sign or message. If you hear something three or more times, think about it and ask yourself, *Is this a sign?* Pay extra attention to whatever it is in your life that marks significant meaning for you. All of these things are there for a reason, and your intuition can act as a guide to bring you greater clarity.

Tuning in to the world of your feelings and intuition can bring you to a richer understanding of your deepest convictions and your true purpose in life—convictions and purpose that go beyond the expectations of your parents, spouse, children, employer, and society.

Through trusting your deepest intuition, you're welcoming growth. If you open yourself up more fully to your intuition and trust now, the messages from Spirit will be there: messages of hope, clarity, and a brighter future; your niche in the universe. And through recognition, introspection, and meditation, you will come to know the power of this gift.

Part II

Achieving Balance—Self-Discovery and Spiritual Illumination

≈ 3 ≈

The Gift of the Fool

In every tarot-card deck, there is a Fool card, which represents a person who is usually depicted as a jovial, fairytale-like, naïve presence. The Fool is often portrayed as being equally proportioned masculine and feminine, and holding unorthodox (nonetheless positive) spiritual attributes, although on the cusp of what some would call naïveté and ignorance. The Fool does not appear to be burdened or worried, but somehow turns inward to his own childlike voice, to his own spirit, to find and live a simple way of being, which is his truth.

The Fool is most often pictured as skipping forward with childlike trust, stepping out over a precipice into the unknown. Similarly, I believe that through Spirit we are each being shown the need to trust in God. Each day, we are given the opportunity to step joyously into the unknown. To do so, we must trust that with each moment in our lives and within each situation, we are divinely being taken care of.

Only one thing in this life is certain: change. No one goes through this life unscarred. You have to trust and know that there is a reason for the fall—a lesson, and an opportunity for growth. When looking at it in a broader perspective, even a fall turns out to be a step on your spiritual journey through this life. You might not understand why at the moment of the fall, but if you trust, then in due time (i.e., in God's time, divine time), you will see more clearly and understand the grand scheme of things.

In feng shui (discussed in detail in Chapter 10), "Tao" means "the path," "the way," or "the principle." Tao is considered in ancient teachings to be the source and guiding principle of all reality and the process of nature by which all things in reality change. When this "way" is followed, it brings about a life of harmony. In short, the Tao comprises both universal wholeness and personal wholeness. The primary principle of the Tao is to be in balance with the universe by flowing with its changes— by being led by and in touch with one's intuition and by trusting fully in the Tao, as one makes increasingly "conscious" choices. Living in the Tao feels to me like living a peaceful, harmonious, universal existence—living in harmony with the totality of change. And that sort of life—living in a spontaneous, flowing-with-change manner—is depicted (in the more "enlightened" reading of tarot cards) as the life of the Fool.

How can we become the Fool? The answer starts with *detachment from outcomes.* That is, it is wise to detach yourself from the outcome of your "footwork." Your responsibility is to take one day at a time and one step at a time, putting one foot in front of the other. Orchestrating the "results" of your footwork is in God's/Spirit's hands, not yours. It's like hiking up a mountain: it's much better to be concentrated on (and enjoying) each step than to be continually looking up at the peak where you think you should be. Focus instead on your intention and what *is*— this very moment—before you. "Future focus"—focusing on the peak—can be hazardous; you might overlook an "obstacle" in your way, stumble over it, and (literally or figuratively) split your lip open! The Fool hikes for the sake of hiking, without worrying about what is at the top or why he isn't there already. The Fool, therefore, truly enjoys the hike.

If I had a dollar for each time someone called me naïve, I'd be very rich. My mother even used to call me that, and I was still a child! I believe that what comes across as my being naïve is really my sensitivity to negative energies in the world. I can't make sense of negativity. I believe in the goodness of all people and situations. I believe in the "karma" and rightness of things, where I know that I can just trust Life/God/Spirit, and everything will work out as it should.

I tell my clients, my friends, and my children to be innocent, to practice innocence, and always have faith. And always, always *love*, for in the beginning there was the love of God for all Creation. To be the Fool is to start from the beginning, to start with a sense of purity and faithful trust.

This is where your intentions come back into play. As a Feng Shui Master, as a Spiritual Intuitive, and as a nurse, I teach that every thought you have possesses energy. This is true for everyone, no matter what their occupation and no matter what their religion. A thought is, at its core, a uniquely sculpted form of energy, *made by you*. I believe we each have the power within ourselves to create healing thoughts, and to make a world of peace and beauty. And this starts with our thoughts and our intentions. Have you ever heard someone exclaim, "She has a very strong will!"? Typically, this kind of statement refers to people who use their thoughts and their intentions *combined with* their determination (or their stubbornness) to set into motion what they truly desire. I believe that we all have the capacity to manifest our thoughts, and that we are doing so every day!

Therefore, examine your thoughts; *really* think about what you intend to have happen in your life. Voice your intentions. Become aware of whether you are wasting energy by thinking negative or superficial thoughts. For example, you're wasting energy if you're swimming in a pool of fear and worry. Anything that you fear becomes a negative thought, which creates a negative intention, which in turn creates a negative experience. Snap yourself out of this! Stop yourself every time you say or think something negative out of fear. Fear of poverty, fear of betrayal, fear of illness—all of these cause us to spend time worrying. Replace these fearful thoughts with prayers, affirmations (see Chapter 14, "The Gift of Affirmations"), meditations, and visualizations about what you really *do* want. Consciously deepen—through affirmations, meditation, reflection, and prayer—your faith in the Gift of Spirit, your trust in God, and then demonstrate it and live it on a daily basis.

Be brave and move forward knowing that you are fully supported by God, and know that there are many blessings upon your path. Have you heard it said that God protects fools and small children? I believe the Fool is a sacred child of God. Self-discovery is the first wondrous element of becoming the Fool. You have the opportunity to start fresh and leave behind patterns of thinking and being that clearly do not serve your highest good. Accessing the Fool within you is the beginning. It is the "start" position in the game of life.

Use your thoughts and intentions in positive ways. Say affirmations like, "I fully desire, want, deserve and intend to have a better job." (Fill in *relationship*, or *living situation*, or whatever applies to you). "I am open; help me receive a job (or whatever) that empowers me and serves me, my family, and others in the highest way." And with these intentions and the energy set forth, with each choice, you will be creating your new, more desirable reality.

What leads you to enlightenment quickest is being conscious of your choices and choosing love and goodness with each step that you take. Come and step into a sense of wonder. *Dare to be the Fool!*

◈ 4 ◈

The Gift of Manifestation

Y ou can manifest peace and happiness. You can manifest true love, prosperity, and health. You can
manifest dreams coming true and have the "happily ever
after" you've always dreamt of.

Here is a formula for manifesting "happily ever after"
in this lifetime:

Karma + feng shui + fate or destiny + right mindset +
right conduct + right speech = "happily ever after"

With this formula, and with a purity of will, strength
and determination, you can manifest anything you wish,
anything your heart desires. It is with a focused will that
new and positive beginnings can be brought forward.
And it is with a state of maturity, summoned with the
knowledge that we are able to direct our lives, that we
come into an awareness of what we truly want in our lives
. . . and then manifest it.

Karma, Feng Shui, and Fate/Destiny

When I speak of karma in this formula, it is simply what
is spoken of in all religions, in every walk of life: In the
Bible's New Testament, Book of Galatians, Paul states,
"Be not deceived: God is not mocked, for whatsoever a

man soweth, that he shall also reap." What you give is what you get. What goes around comes around. This is the divine law of cause and effect, where every action produces a specific reaction. How you live today—your thoughts, your words, your actions—affect the state of your present reality today, and these same actions produce consequences that will affect your tomorrow. Behind karma is "cosmic law": we must account for and be responsible for all of our behaviors. Gaining self-mastery and understanding the basic dynamic of karma are essential elements of creating and manifesting our reality.

Feng shui is covered in detail in Chapter 10, so for now I'll simply provide a basic definition: Feng shui is the ancient Oriental art of balancing, harmonizing, and enhancing the flow of natural energy. It is about living consciously on this earth, becoming truly aware of your surroundings so that you may enjoy and really live the highest quality of life. We eat certain foods to make us feel good; or we get a massage; or we work out, do yoga, or sit and meditate. All of these activities alter the energy in our body in positive ways, which we can directly feel. Feng shui brings the same principle to our surroundings. By being more aware of our surroundings, we can be more cognizant of the energy around us, whether it be positive or negative; and then we can make the adjustments needed to change the energy to reflect what we truly want to be surrounded by.

The divine laws at work in karma and feng shui gracefully bring us to another facet of the "happily ever after" manifestation formula: our fate, our destiny. For simplicity's sake, think of fate or destiny as a predetermined "blueprint" or as certain inevitable life circumstances.

But we have the ability to *oversee the direction* of how we build our lives from this blueprint.

The circumstances of our origin generate our fate. And although we cannot go back and change these circumstances, we *can* influence our fate according to how we react and respond to our life situations. That is not to say we should not ask, "*How did this deplorable situation happen to me*" and genuinely feel like it is a horrible "fate" that you are a part of. But in the face of adversity—what seems like an unjust fate—you may find forces that help you understand the true message behind your fate. This deeper understanding can give you strength and encouragement to go on forward and build your life to reflect goodness and positive manifestation.

Right Mindset, Right Conduct, and Right Speech

When I speak of "right" in this formula, I mean "good" or "positive." Manifesting the life you've always dreamt of starts with your mindset. When you possess the "right" mindset, you are exhibiting a *positive* mindset, *positive* views, and *positive* meditation. We are all capable of discerning what is "right" versus what is "wrong" in our mindset, conduct, and speech. Right thinking leads to right action, which leads to manifesting positive developments.

"Right conduct" equates with actions that we can personally *and* objectively judge as being positive. Do your actions convey love? Kindness? Self-truth? Do your actions reflect living in goodness and beauty, and a reverence for life? Do your actions follow your passions? Conduct plus passion equals prosperity. Following your passion will lead to prosperity: perhaps monetary prosperity, but at the very least the intangible prosperity that fills one's heart beyond what words can describe. Right conduct leads to manifesting abundance on all levels—material, emotional, and spiritual—including rich life experiences. In fact, as I write this I have tapped into a well-spring of love and passion. My heart feels so full, knowing that I am following my passion and sharing what I have come to realize is my gift to share with this world.

When I refer to "right speech" in the formula, I always think of the Don Miguel Ruiz book *The Four Agreements*, specifically his chapter on speech—how your thoughts are undoubtedly and perfectly put into words. Believe in your word; be true to your word; be impeccable with your word. Being conscious of and using your words to not only communicate, but also to summon universal support will help smooth the way as you move forward in the process of manifesting your intentions, your goals, and your dreams.

By breaking down this formula into these separate elements, we can become truly aware of our lives, and through this new knowledge and understanding, make the necessary steps toward the great gift of manifestation.

Believe, Deserve, and Have Faith

There are three main concepts to draw upon for the energy of manifestation. More detail about each component follows the list:

> *Believe.* Truly believe in what you desire or dream of. Feel it, know it without an ounce of doubt. Know that, with God, all things are possible.

Deserve. Know that you are worthy of manifesting this desire or dream; really know that you deserve the pure goodness of it. Have confidence in what you believe to be your truth, and stay strong and true in your convictions to manifest it. Deserving something automatically facilitates confidence.

Have faith. Recognize that the Source (God) that can supply the manifestation of your desire or dream is far greater than yourself, and has a divine plan for the manifestation of the highest good in this world. Have faith that your heartfelt desire is part of that divine plan. Holding fast to faith can be a saving grace for someone who lacks clarity or is in a state of weakness and uncertainty. There is an affirmation prayer (see Chapter 14 for more on the concept) that I have memorized from an old Mass candle of mine: "Blessed Lady of Charity, please give me the strength and shield me against all enemies. Holy Lady of Charity, I humbly and fervently ask that my prayers be heard and answered. I thank thee for all thy infinite goodness. Bless me. In *faith*, amen." After I recite that affirmation, I continue to pray and petition to God to continue to buoy my faith, to help me stay strong and true to my convictions.

Believe

I believe in anything that I feel is true for me. And I mean I *really believe*. I always buy Lucky Charms cereal in March because of St. Patrick's Day. I believe that Lucky Charms are indeed "magically delicious," but I really associate eating them with being magical and lucky. As I enjoy my bowl, sitting alone, nestled against the arm of the couch, I think positive thoughts and open my heart and mind to the magic of life and to being or feeling lucky. And so I *am* lucky, because I *believe* I am!

Believing and understanding the power of your thoughts is the key to your life. Remaining optimistic and filled with faith will attract the right energies to you, which will, in turn, attract the right opportunities to you. This is called the Divine Law of Attraction. Your thoughts and the words you speak become your intentions. And your intentions become your life, your reality. Thus, your beliefs and intentions actually manifest your desires and your dreams.

Deserve

I deserve only good things in my life. I am worthy of a Mercedes Benz, and I have been since I was old enough to drive. I am worthy of healthy, whole, loving relationships. I am worthy of that money tree that is in my backyard. My mother and father would always say to me, when I was a very young girl, "Tina thinks there's a money tree in the backyard." And even though I was very young, I responded, "Well, yes; yes, there is." I have always thought of money as energy, even as a young girl. I fully deserve a "happily ever after" and I'm going to have one. I have always felt deserving of good things, despite any adversity. And so good things have found their way to me, always!

Many people don't feel that they are truly worthy or deserving of good in their lives. People who are already not feeling worthy are prone to fall in line with how others will define them or how others are going to feel in reference to *their* thoughts and choices. This creates a nondeserving double whammy. They ultimately end up putting others' opinions and beliefs about what's right above their own.

I am here to tell you that we all *do* deserve to have it *all!* And the "all" has a different meaning for each of us. It entails our own personal truth. We do deserve to have the life we've always dreamt of having, and a chance at having the peace we've always longed for. Sometimes when we lack clarity we ask questions like, *Am I really at the right place in my life? Am I on the right path? Why is there such a struggle while living in this world? What do I feel I deserve for myself to be truly happy? Should I go this way or that way?* One way or another, we will surrender and stop resisting. We will stop asking questions and struggling over our own personal truth. For some it will be through emotionally or physically breaking down; for others it will be through "seeing the light" or a spiritual awakening. We each have the power to listen to Spirit through signs, thoughts, and intuition. We each have power to then turn inward and find the answers that we seek— answers that will inevitably lead us to clarity and build a foundation of confidence within us. The following diary entry shows how Spirit turned my sadness to encouragement by revealing to me that I *do* deserve to have it all; that I *am* worthy.

Diary Entry: March 23, 2006

I sat on the floor in my bedroom against the side of my bed in front of my nightstand, almost hugging the nightstand, hunched over, holding my knees. I was in a depressed state, contemplating, thinking, solemn. "I miss you, Daddy," I said aloud with a sad and lonely whisper.

Immediately, the left side of my entire body was covered with huge goose bumps, and I physically felt his presence on the left side of me. He got real close and very slowly said, "I'm here, baby . . . you are going to have it all . . . and you . . . deserve it all." Immediately, the goose bumps that covered my left side vanished. And I experienced a true moment of peace. I felt reassured and deserving. When I need Spirit, it is there. I can feel it, see it, hear it, and sense it.

We can start today, at this moment, by using our thoughts in positive ways and by shaping our intentions. We can affirm to ourselves, "I fully desire, deserve, and intend to have a better job that serves myself and others to the highest good." The same applies to relationships, children, family, money, etc. You can simply fill in the blank as it pertains to your life. And with these intentions, the support of Spirit and the energy set forth, you are opening the gates to move forward in your life. With each moment and with each choice, you are creating your new reality. You are now moving ahead through the use of the Divine Law of Attraction!

Be aware of what you truly desire, what you truly want in your life. Find time to contemplate and meditate upon your deepest desire. Focus on what you truly want to have happen in your life, and see if there are any self-sabotaging thoughts or practices that are keeping you from moving forward. Know that you deserve a new beginning, new abundance on all levels, and "a new lease on life." Setting goals and putting forth your intentions moves you straight into positive growth, into an opening of your heart, and ultimately, into experiencing happiness and a world of delight.

Have Faith

Have faith in God's power to keep you safe, protected, and provided for. Avoid negative people, thoughts, and situations. Negativity will only block you and push away your good manifesting energy, making it even harder for opportunities to come in.

To buoy your faith does take continual practice. I can vouch for that. It's easy to get submerged in fear. But the only power your fear has is the power you give it. Set your fear aside; envision yourself handing it away. Raise your hand and say, "Hey, here you go. You can have it. Goodbye." You have the power to create a happy and harmonious life. Make the decision now to feel happy, safe, and secure. Know that what you desire most can become a reality . . . *your* reality. Start making conscious choices and conscious decisions. Choose your most heartfelt, positive thoughts *right now.*

Hold fast to your faith. Practice praying, meditating, journaling, doing yoga/exercise, eating healthfully, reciting positive affirmations, and holding on to your visions. Stay true to your convictions and who you want to become. I am a huge fan of affirmations (positive statements): written ones, posted all over the house, and those spoken aloud. You have to drive the positive statements into your mind. Practice this. Pray this. And it will be.

Visualization is another extremely important dynamic in the grand scheme of manifestation. It is an added sensory input that engenders a magnetic attraction to your beliefs. Writing this book, I have used visualization from day one. I see and hold a very strong vision of this book. It is a beautifully covered book, outlined in gleaming light. I see the title on it. I even see that little round sticker on the cover of the book that says "Oprah's Book Club." In order to attract what you want, you have to see it, experience it, and connect with it. To attract the right agent and publisher for my book, I visualized not just an agent. I visualized Spirit sending me *the most fantastic* agent and publisher to represent my book. And in my vision that agent and publisher call me to say, "Tina . . . You had me at hello."

The Gift of Manifestation is the gift of manifesting miracles, both big and small. Ask for a miracle, let go of all ideas of *how* you think it should appear, and one miracle will be coming right up, just like you ordered it off of a fancy dinner menu. Don't worry about who's cooking it or how much it costs; just know it will appear before you on a beautiful piece of fine china lined with silver and gold.

∞ 5 ∞

The Gift of Marriage

Right now I'm thinking, *Ah, man . . . does Spirit really want me to write a chapter on relationships?* Why does the word "relationship" cause such stirrings in one's heart? It's because the art of relationship is about being vulnerable. It's about opening oneself up to the wonders of love's light *and* the wonders of darkness, the wonders of joy *and* the wonders of pain.

Marriage without inner wholeness (i.e., the kind that many people find themselves in today), without a true inner marriage, can feel like a life sentence in prison. We can feel despair, stuck and desperate. That's why *Desperate Housewives* has been such a big hit! There's a reason they don't call it *Enlightened Housewives*. We are *all* desperate at one point or another, and all of us have experienced "issues" with our relationships.

I believe there is great danger in not recognizing the social conditioning that goes along with many of today's marital standards. These standards are often not congruent with the inner standards of our true selves. To me, the most important aspect of any marriage is the efficacy of your own inner values and your inner marriage—the marriage to oneself. A good and whole marriage starts with inner marriage, but how do we define, balance, and nurture our inner marriage properly, and yet still be united in a whole marriage today?

What are we truly looking for? So many of us wander this earth in search of purpose and happiness, only to get caught in a maze of false images, of ego, and societal illusions. And we like to drag somebody along with us . . . or be dragged along. I believe what we are searching for is our truth. I love when the lead character in the movie *Jerry Maguire* says, "You complete me." However, what we *really* need to do is stand in front of the mirror, point to ourselves, and say, "*You* complete me."

When you come to know, firsthand, the pain and darkness that can come from being a partner in a relationship that ends or is dysfunctional, you *can* experience great upheaval, difficulty, and darkness . . . to the point of feeling stripped of everything, both materially and emotionally, leaving you feeling raw. But then, after all of the pain and the crippling despair, a few words of hope from deep within can emerge, lifting you up like a sacred line to the divine.

With your willingness to experience the darkness in a relationship comes the opportunity to connect with yourself and with the merging of lightness and darkness within you and without you—to know both your own divine strengths and human weaknesses, as well as those of all others, including your partner's. With a vision of what is true and sacred to you (the "highest good"), a well-nurtured faith in oneself and Spirit/God, and a persevering intention to realize that vision, you will come to more fully and wholly love yourself. Only then will you be able to truly love and merge with another. A sacred line will be formed between you and your exalted love.

I like to envision it as a line of "fairy dust," tying your two souls into the shape of an infinity sign. The true love from within and the true love from another can bring you ecstasy, power, and light.

Inner Marriage, Outer Marriage, and Sacred Marriage

Here is a formula for creating a sacred and whole marriage:

Inner marriage (within—to Spirit/God/Self) + outer marriage (without—to another individual) = sacred marriage

Inner Marriage

Today it seems that there is little nurturing of a spiritual kind, little enchantment and sacredness in the typical marriage/relationship. Add to this the responsibilities of children, finances, home mortgages, and keeping up with the Joneses, and it's no wonder there is a prescription-drug problem (let alone an illegal-drug problem) in our society. It's a ready-made plan for "Triple-D Disease": Death of Love, Disaster of the Heart, and a Devastating Divorce/Loss. What many of us really seem to be missing is the freedom and the wellness that come from having a healthy and sacred relationship. On a soul level, to some relationships can feel like entrapment, with a good chance that one or both individuals will lose their individuality and thereby feel disempowered, scared, and resentful.

In relationships, all of us come to the table with aspects of ourselves that are like inner wounds—power struggles, control issues, or abandonment issues, just to name a few— or patterns of both constructive traits and destructive traits. These may be patterns such as attracting abusive partners or taking in addicts or "energy suckers" who drain you emotionally, financially, or spiritually (or all three at the same time). These inner issues influence how we see both ourselves and our "significant other," whether we mean for them to or not. Upon meeting a relationship partner, we see two kinds of characteristics: 1) those that would allow us to bring balance into our relationship or 2) the characteristics *in ourselves* that need to come out from their hiding places in the dark, unconscious parts of ourselves for healing and releasing— *for the betterment of ourselves*. Either way, these characteristics are being mirrored for one's higher learning and healing. But here's the deceptive part: if you don't realize what you yourself bring to the table, you will keep repeating the same old, worn-out (and possibly very painful) patterns. You will keep attracting the same relationship, one after another, until you finally realize that you do not have a whole *inner* marriage.

Okay, so where do we start? We must first become aware of and acknowledge our inner marriage. So many of my clients want to meet "the one"—their "soul mate." They say that they're tired of waiting and want to know when "the one" is coming. They want to know what Spirit Guidance and feng shui cures they can implement immediately to find "the one." And in their panic and their anxiety, some have even asked me what specific day and time "the one" is coming. I'd really like to smack them upside the head or shake them and say, "*You* are the one!"

Inner marriage is simple (though not necessarily easy)—after all, it is about you. Yes, *all about you*. When you love yourself, there is a simple joy of self-acceptance.

And this joy is what radiates outward to attract a "kindred spirit" to you.

Building one's inner marriage requires conscious preparation to get to a realm of self-identity where there is a sacred "gateway," the source of the urge to merge with another. In other words, you must prepare your heart to receive someone. Love is a cornerstone of our existence, and preparation for that existence is key, whether we are alone—in order to discover our own inner marriage—or whether we are in the exploration phase within a relationship.

Pray. Ask God and Spirit to open your heart and make clear what is not whole, and what is in need of healing. Do you need to forgive someone or forgive yourself? Do you need to set boundaries of any kind, including boundaries of integrity that reflect your self-worth?

Allow yourself to become open and heal from past relationship traumas and upsets. Recognize the patterns and lessons from those past events that no longer serve your higher purpose, so that you can stop repeating them. If you don't learn and grow, you'll draw in another person to repeat what you didn't learn the time before. Allow room for new energy to come in. Let go of any negative emotions like anger, bitterness, or resentment, and just see what happens in your new relationships!

Prepare your home and the space around you, as well, to reflect the highest qualities of your heart energy: open and loving. This can support your undertakings. For example, something I've done myself and that I suggest it to my clients is to make room for "his" car in my garage. Each day, I pull into the side of the garage and allot enough room for "his" vehicle. I have made space in my closet for "his" clothing, and an extra drawer remains empty. I have even bought a spare toothbrush. I am consciously offering up to the "one who Spirit wills for me" a very special, enchanted place, a place for "him" to rest his head and his heart. This preparation allows a form of kindred energy to be released into the universe, and issues a trumpet call heralding "his" arrival.

When you are centered in your inner marriage, you can then freely give fully of yourself in an unconditional way.

Outer Marriage

Before you bring yourself to the relationship table, it is good to ask yourself, *What do I truly want in a partner?* Write down your honest, thoughtful answers. If you're asking me, I want a self-confident, sexy, athletic type who balances my eccentricities and quirks. I want a man who can coexist in a spiritual, higher, soul-growing kind of love. Never having had a close girlfriend/best friend, I look to my partner to also be my best friend—trusting, playful, honest, and true. A best friend who is my lover: that's what I want in a partner—someone to share in the fun and excitement of this lifetime . . . a hand to hold while skipping down life's pathway, through the good times amongst the rainbows and butterflies, and a hand that will hold me tight through the bad, dark times. This is what I believe in. This is what I am worthy of. And I have learned that it's a waste of my life to settle for less. Even though we may not realize it, we all yearn for a real "enchanted" kind of love—to be a part of a sacred, loving relationship in which you not only feel passion and a sense of discovery, but you also honor and claim a stake in the emotional ground that you both are committed to standing upon. I think we all want a love that is true, rising above the "societal-casual-superficial" kind of relationship. Now that you've worked on your inner marriage, you can buck the trend of the majority of relationships today, which seem so often to be run by negative programming, convenience, and routine (like the participants are a couple of robots). So, *what do you want?*

Now at the table, with our inner marriage in check, and our reservation for an outer marriage, we feel whole, ready and open to receive love. We feel this overflowing love, love for the self, love for the universe and are ready to focus and channel this love into another human being.

The coming of this new and beautiful relationship, where the two people enter, combining their energies and their love, creating a third energy—that of the sacred marriage itself—forms a relationship where each individual expresses the highest and most creative aspects of themselves.

Sacred Marriage

A sacred marriage is a sacred balance. Making the most of the Gift of Marriage takes conscious and continual effort, through both intention and actions, day by day and moment by moment, to balance the equation:

Inner marriage + outer marriage = sacred marriage

Every moment offers an opportunity to bring gratitude forward into your life, and a chance to bring love and truth to the table. *What will you be serving? What will you be receiving?*

Being in a sacred marriage feels like true bliss: it's ecstatically delightful; it's euphoric to the nth degree; it's magical and truly wonderful! It brings forward such goodness and peace! It feels like the sun bursting forth with love and real light as each partner feels both the pleasure of being nourished and the pleasure of nourishing.

Time is one of the most underestimated aspects of the art of relationships. Time does heal all wounds. Time lets us heal, nurse our wounds, pack them with gauze, suture them up, rub salve all over them, and wait. And if we work toward living in goodness, time will unfold the mystery. In the Gift of Marriage, time will tell everything. One day, you will find a person to offer an exchange of salve for each other's wounds, and you will have come into a place of healing and unconditional love.

How do we know we have found a sacred marriage? I've held an image in my mind for the past five years, and have even integrated this vision into the work I've done with my clients. The image is from one of my oracle cards representing a relationship that is spiritually based, with both partners having true faith and profound, spiritually principled beliefs. I have always been drawn to the beauty and perfection of the image: two dolphins are perfectly entwined, two beams of light spiraling around them in the sea, with subtler light rays radiating down from the water's surface. I think of this image while holding in mind the image of the man who stands before me (as a possible partner for me or for a client), and I ask myself, *Is this a sacred partner?* I then "tune in" and listen to what my heart says. When it says *yes*, it feels like a deeply inhaled breath of peace. And I can see the two people (either he and I or he and my client) transposed onto the image of the dolphins. And when my heart says *no*, it feels like an immediate and distinct disconnect . . . *or* an "Uh, hmmm, I'm not quite sure, I don't know, maybe"— that is, clearly, some doubt! So, as an exercise or practice for yourself, look at the person or visualize the person you're considering as a partner, then ask yourself, *Is this my partner in a sacred marriage . . . in a grand, enchanted fairy-tale adventure?* And then listen to the answer from within you, where Spirit speaks to each of us.

I often follow with more questions on this sacred quest. Just like the previously mentioned image of the dolphins, does my body wrap around his—a melting together that can only be described as safety and peace, ecstasy and rapture? Does my brain wrap around his—with intellect and understanding? Does my heart wrap around his—with a peaceful sense of trust, compassion, and an enchanted realm that is reserved for our love to grow?

There are other questions that I've asked myself and have raised to clients in their quest to find true love and a sacred marriage. I often hear my clients say that they don't respect their partner. And in spiritual terms, that means there is no reverence there. The difference is that respect is of the ego and judgment whereas reverence derives from respect, a respect of the heart, a deep love and compassion without judgment. So, if you're in a relationship, ask yourself: *Do I revere this person? And does this person revere me? Do I feel cherished and do I cherish this person?*

Taking a look at judgment, again, can we look at how our inner and outer marriages come together, forming the sacred marriage? Might I approach my partner-to-be and state, "Hello. Here are my darknesses and my weaknesses. I'm happy to meet your darknesses and weaknesses. Can we learn, play, and grow with one another while we illuminate our falsities together and become enlightened?"

When you are in a sacred marriage, you have a feeling that you have received something from God, a blessing from the Holy Spirit. The touch of your Beloved's hand holds a power that denotes a feeling of being godsent . . . and that this love strengthens and expands the will of God. There comes a point (and I've experienced this firsthand) when you realize that merging with another soul would positively expand your existence, and better the world and humanity as a whole.

When you find a partner who, when you're with them, makes you ask, *How can we bless the world together by having found each other?* then you know you have found a relationship worthy of a sacred marriage.

⁓ 6 ⁓

The Gift of Children

Pregnancy and birthing provide the opportunity to experience one's true inner connection to the Source (God) and personal power. It is an amazing opportunity to experience empowerment as a woman and to connect with the Gift of Spirit. From the time of conception, through gestation, to the moment of your baby's arrival, a whole world of self-discovery is made available to you, which can illuminate much about the divinity of who you are and the sacredness of life.

Childbirth

From my own experience, I learned that the first step in recognizing the Gift of Children was to set aside my "programming" about pregnancy and the birthing process—the programming handed down in the sometimes-horrible stories that family and friends pass along about their own childbirth experiences, inclusive of the whining, suffering, drama, and trauma; the programming set from watching movies that always seem to portray the birthing process in a negative light. All of this programming sets forth the idea that pregnancy is a time of misery, great danger, worry, and unpredictability.

Empowering Birth

The mind has great power. Give yourself kind thoughts about a beautiful birth. I've enjoyed all three of my pregnancies. But if I'd had this chapter to read, I would have had a much better time with the first two. I was most scared the first time—terrified, actually. It made for a not-so-perfect delivery. I had rushed to the hospital the moment I felt a contraction, got hooked up to the IVs and monitors, which made it all the more unsettling and unnatural, and proceeded to have a very long and intense labor of eighteen hours.

Here are considerations for an empowering pregnancy and birth:

Savor all of the emotions that come with pregnancy. Celebrate the changes your body undergoes, without being harsh on yourself. Really enjoy the nourishment of eating for two. Listen to what your body craves with an attitude of healthiness and moderation, and enjoy a healthy weight gain.

Journal through your pregnancy and birthing. I believe journaling is a self-healing practice throughout life. Keeping a pregnancy journal also makes for an amazing read in years to come.

Always be positive with your words. Practice positivity. If you feel negative or angry words coming through your mind and slipping right off your tongue, make a conscious effort to offset those with positive words.

Talk to your baby. Meditate, be still, and speak to your baby both in your mind and aloud, connecting your spirits. I believe babies can sense this emotional and spiritual connection, and that it makes them develop better, stronger, and healthier.

Know that the quality of care you receive is of the highest importance. Also, the more education you have about the birthing process, the better off you'll be. Prenatal nutrition, massage, yoga, exercise, spas, adequate rest, vacations, and nesting in preparation for your child are all extremely vital to a healthy, holistic pregnancy and birth.

Labor

Unfortunately for me, I didn't understand the concept of turning my birthing into total personal power until the third time. Labor is ultimately between the mother and her baby. Believe this sentence. What I call "the others"—your physician, midwife, husband or partner, family, and friends, are there only to offer you and your baby support.

Inside of you is the power to have a peaceful birth, naturally, like God intended it to be. There is no need to lash out at anyone like we see in the movies! This only wastes good, precious energy that you need for the baby. Lashing out and acting out of fear creates emotional and spiritual distance, not connection, between you and your baby.

Trust that you know how to give birth; listen to and connect with your body. *Focus inside*. Send the baby messages of reassurance. The effects of your thoughts can have profound effects on your body's systems, such as blood pressure and pulse, which will have either a positive or negative effect on your baby. During birthing the baby is still part of your body, so make every effort to tune into and be supportive and loving toward the baby.

Let your baby know that he is safe, and when it's time, tell him that it is okay for him to come out—that he will be fine. Certainly the pain of labor is a signal that says, "Stop what you are doing and focus on this pain—focus, and use these contractions and listen to your body."

Allow the labor. Women in labor must *allow* the pain and make it part of the process. Flailing about does not help. Screaming obscenities certainly does not help. *Going deep within does—connecting to this creation*. Concentrate and focus on your body and your cervix. Let your cervix open for your baby's head and body. Visualize this opening and birthing happening. Dive down into the contractions and let them pass over you, like you're diving and swimming in a magnificent ocean. Giving birth isn't easy, but to stay in a state of grace instead of resisting is such an amazingly rewarding process. *Be courageous*. By being courageous, you will have the greatest opportunity to feel your own true power and connection with Spirit.

To Doula or Not to Doula?

A doula is a woman who supports you through your pregnancy and your birthing. She is a person who is experienced with all stages of birthing and will help educate you with a birthing plan. She will support you, leading you through the most positive birthing experience you can imagine.

My suggestion, from experience, is that if a suitable doula is available, you should get her and use her. It is very much worth it. You might think you do not really need one or you do not want to spend the extra money, and there might even be an issue with your spouse or partner not approving of one. But a supportive, most gracious birth outcome is being more readily assured by having a doula. Hence, the value of having a doula is priceless.

Upon meeting with a doula, you will know immediately if she is right for you. This is a great way to exercise your own intuition for your and your baby's highest good. If you do not feel she's the one, continue to interview until you do find the one who is.

I would never have had such a special and amazing third birthing experience without my doula. I can look back and say how incredibly grateful I am that she came into my life for the birth of my child. To finally have the wisdom and courage to experience natural childbirth the third time around with that unfailing support was truly empowering. Throughout the labor, I could hear her words, and I focused on what she was saying and on internalizing them to my baby. I looked into my doula's eyes, which reassured me that it was okay, that I was safe. And with that reassurance, I pushed my final two pushes for my angel baby, Steven Joseph, named after my brother, to enter the world. That birth had an unspoken radiance of love, light, and pure grace that would make for a place of safety and empowerment for any mother.

(Special thanks to my doula, Deanna Pamies, and midwife, Barbara Dembeck, in St. Augustine Beach, Florida.)

Raising Your Child

The subject of children is very near and dear to my heart. I have been blessed with three beautiful children thus far, and they have truly been a gift of God's Grace to me. Before jumping straight into a discussion about the Gift of Children, however, I want to remind you that you were once a child. In Chapter 3, "The Gift of the Fool," I speak of the fool as a sacred child of God. I believe that at the core of who we are, there is a child, wrapped like an infant, in a continual process of creation. Each one of us has a child within who is continually unfolding like a flower.

Breaking the Cycle

Due to the fact that much of our "present-moment awareness" is influenced by the largely unconscious beliefs and
emotional attachments we formed as children, it can be
hard, at times, to separate ourselves from the "programming" of our own childhood. For me, the number-one
concept that is crucial for you to understand—and, more
importantly, to believe—is that our parents did the best
they could, and that they were taught by their parents,
who did the best that *they* could, etc., etc. The point is
simple, really. If they knew better or could have done better, they would have. And so we were raised, and now we
are here at this juncture in our lives, and we need to rise
up and make a *choice* to apply our conscious awareness
and understanding to break the cycle of blindly mimick-
ing the way our parents raised us.

We as parents, as adults, as community leaders, as
teachers, as healers, as citizens, need to communicate
clearly with love and wisdom to our children, whether
or not we got that kind of treatment from our parents!
Many people were raised in a seemingly unending cycle
of fear based on old patterns of disempowerment, neglect,
abandonment, abuse, and the displacement of negative
emotions. We need to stop the cycle of handing down
this emotional garbage to yet another generation. It is
time to rethink, relearn, and renew a positive way of life
to comfort, nurture, and guide our children. Kindness
and compassion need to replace any anger and superior-
ity that your parents may have raised you with. Honesty,
integrity, and responsibility have to be role-modeled if we
want our children to see how we can all make the world
a better place. No matter how you were brought up, you

must do everything that you possibly can to make your child see the world as a place of love.

Teach your children to have an open and loving heart and, most of all, to believe that they hold the power inside of them to heal themselves as well as others. Help them to believe in and use "fairy dust" (my visualization and metaphor for healing and expressing soft, tender love and sparkling delight) just as much as you guide them to believe in Santa Claus. There is so much love and healing that they can do with fairy dust. Teach them to send it out to someone in need of healing and love. I teach my own children to visualize and use fairy dust like the Fairy Godmother in *Cinderella*, the way she twirled her wand that spewed a glittering trail of light. I teach them that this visualization method can help people heal on all levels and generate a feeling of peace.

Teach your children to empower themselves. Teach them to express themselves directly and openly, but with kindness, paying special attention to the power of the spoken word. One day I was picking up my daughter, Taylor, from school—she was in kindergarten at the time—and she ran up to me saying, "Mom, you were right, the bully girl yelled at me, really ugly again, and in a mean voice, 'What are you looking at?!' and I said back to her what you told me to say: 'Oh, I just think you are a pretty girl and I know there is a nice girl inside you.' All of a sudden, the bully girl changed her attitude toward me and actually didn't say anything for a second." I explained to my daughter that the bully girl might have emotional problems at home and that she's only crying out for love.

It's imperative that we teach our children how not to take things personally. Problems from other kids are just that—their own problems, their own garbage. And in order for our children to learn this concept, we have to lead by example! By looking at how much we react to what other people say or do to us, we can gauge how much we might need to work on letting go of our concern for what is truly other people's business. I also recommend reading Don Miguel Ruiz's *The Four Agreements,* mentioned earlier, which addresses the lesson of not taking things personally. One day when Taylor was in the first grade, she got into the car and said, "The teacher put the nastiest girl right behind me! And I know, Mom . . . I know what you're going to say: that she is there on purpose so that I can send her love, fairy dust, and pink light into her heart."

Another example of using words for good came one Sunday afternoon while I was taking my kids shopping at a huge warehouse store. As we were browsing and shopping, we came to the frozen-food aisles. There were two older ladies with a tasting table set up, and they were offering food samples while talking amongst themselves. As we passed by, they offered us samples of yogurt smoothies. Taylor, who was nine years old at this time, responded, "Yes, please." She reached out for the sample, ate it, made eye contact with the ladies, and with an earnest voice said, "That was really good. Thank you, and I hope you have a nice day." The two ladies were surprised and delighted. They turned to me and said that after working there for a year, not one child has responded with a gracious "thank you" like that. I was overwhelmed with joy at hearing this. I seized the opportunity to reiterate to my daughter how positive and powerful her spoken word can be. This was a small example, yet a rewarding moment for me as a parent.

What and how we speak to our children is of the utmost importance. What we say gets carved into their minds. Reflect for a moment on what you remember from your own childhood, and you will begin to understand that parents are a primary vehicle for knowledge, wisdom, and cultivation to children in their young years.

I most certainly can remember what was said to me when I was a child. I remember some negative sentences that are still etched in my brain. On the other hand, I can tell you today that I still remember the positive things that were said to me, too. My mother's best friend, Mary Sibley, who was like a mother to me for many years, would always tell me in a soft, sincere voice, "Tina, you're a sweet, sweet girl." I can literally still hear her voice; I hung on to those kind words. We need to remember these statements and events from our own childhood to break any negative cycle. Many parents have told me they've more than once stopped themselves and said or thought, "Oh, my God, I'm turning into my mother" or "I sounded just like my father."

Teaching Children about Goodness

Doing good deeds and being of service to others are among the most valuable qualities that you can imprint on your child's character. My daughter has a very light marking on her face, similar to a birthmark. It started like a puppy-dog patch under her right eye. By the time she was six, it had become a distinct shape—like that of Africa—that now covers the right side of her face. She is now twelve, and feels proud of herself and her relationship to this mark because we came together to realize that the meaning for this marking is that she and I have a special purpose in Africa. We both believe that we have a calling to go to Africa to do work and be of service. We started researching and began writing a plan for the building of fresh-water wells in areas where such work can be done cost-effectively, as well as providing clothing and shoes to children in need. We both excitedly look forward to starting this philanthropic work together. And she feels remarkably special that her unique physical characteristic has given her, at such a young age, a grander feeling of imparting goodness, a remarkably positive sense of responsibility, and a life lesson of people coming together in the world like a family.

By setting a platform for children's spirits to dance, they shall inherit the earth and the earth will grow toward peace. This is the pathway to a future of greater understanding in the family of humankind and peace on the planet.

Communication

Children are not born with a fully developed ability to voice their feelings verbally. The ability to express oneself through verbal communication is a skill we must teach them and guide them through, using different modes of communication to see what fits each child best.

It's also important to explain to children the why of things that happen, at least to the best of our ability: the *why* of separation or divorce, the *why* of a serious illness, or the *why* of death. By offering our children demonstrations of how we communicate and express ourselves and our emotions at times of important events, we can help them express their own emotions, as well as ensure they can better understand the events of their lives; they will be less inclined to form unreasonable, potentially damaging perspectives about the causes of events, such as blaming themselves for an occurrence totally beyond their control.

Children are often much more resilient and wiser than we give them credit for. Grief and loss, disappointment and frustration are normal parts of life. Helping them acknowledge this and giving them creative and constructive outlets for their emotions is important and helpful for us to do as parents.

One outlet for children is visual art. From crayons to paint-and-easel sets, from scrap-booking to sidewalk chalk, art gives children the ability to express their feelings, both conscious and subconscious—thereby contributing to the development of wholeness (and, if necessary, healing) while they create something self-pleasing and potentially beautiful. Art provides a great channel to support each child's holistic emotional development.

Writing is another outlet. It is incredibly empowering for children to learn how to express themselves through the written word. Writing is a great outlet for expressing feelings and thoughts, while simultaneously freeing up a child's mind space. It can serve as an emotional investigation, so to speak.

Other art forms, such as, dance, music, and theater, can also provide powerful outlets of expression for a child. By providing these outlets, you allow each child to put energy into a talent to express their inner self, while simultaneously having a therapeutic effect.

All of these outlets provide a healthy, safe, and effective release of negative emotions and offer creative motivation, along with an increased sense of well-being and a priceless boost to self-esteem. When you support their creative undertakings, you can unlock and witness their natural exuberance and create a channel of understanding and connection between you and your child.

Children's Intuition

Our children are also a lot more intuitive than we give them credit for. A few weeks before my daughter's third birthday, she came to my bedroom and spoke in a strong voice that demanded my attention. Standing at my bedroom door, she said, "Mother, look at me." I was dusting my dresser, and as I turned my head to make eye contact with her, she said, "Not this birthday, but right after my next birthday, we will have a baby boy and we will name him Frank." I raised one eyebrow, tilted my head, and pursed my lips, trying not to laugh. I just smiled and said in a voice that made it sound like I believed her, "Oh, yeah?! Okay, Taylor, all right, sounds good."

Her birthday was September 3 and that next year, I became pregnant. And so it came to pass after her fourth birthday, on December 12, I gave birth to a baby boy whom we named Frank. Frank was the name of my former husband's father, and December 12 also happened to be Frank Sinatra's birthday. We knew, without a doubt, that this was to be our baby, Frank.

All children are intuitive to some degree; some have more perception than others. Highly intuitive children often exhibit keen and very unique messages with striking accuracy. The key is to stay open-minded to what emerges with your child's intuition. Respecting your child's insights will teach her to trust her own gift of intuition and nurture her own inner compass.

Reflection

Love is the main reason for being a parent. The experience and exchange of love that is available when one becomes a parent is one of life's most beautiful gifts. The bond and connection that is there to be nurtured with one's child can make for a most sacred and amazing relationship.

The gift of my own children has been like a *perfect human creation for my soul to experience*. It is a bond of pure joy, wonder, and amazement . . . a bond of unconditional love, of what can be described only as a sacred connection of *pure love through form*.

I believe that children "choose" their parents on a soul level; and we chose more: our own gender, as well as the culture and time of our descending to the earth plane. I have to tell you that I did not connect to, value, or come to understand this until I experienced firsthand the intuitive and soulful connection of each of my children descending into human form. I strongly felt each of my children in soul form, just before I became pregnant.

Your children are here to teach you, as much as you are here to teach them. Your child has chosen you specifically as a vehicle to come to this earth plane. Not only have they chosen you as a parent, but they in turn can actually be a reflection of you. If we accept this vision of life and seek to grow in understanding of these principles of the soul's choice as it descends and the "equality" of parent-child reflection, we can better develop lasting and healthy relationships between parents and their children.

Here is something I'd like you to think about regarding the reflection of you in your child: Let's say that your child is sick. I would suggest that you take a good look at what the child is going through, and what you (and your spouse, where applicable) are going through in your lives at that particular moment. Something is going on either with the child himself or with the parent whom he is reflecting. Earaches, for example, are a common ailment that can lead to ear infections. Possible cause of earaches from a "reflection" point of view is that the child is hearing something he doesn't want to: parents arguing, siblings fighting, kids at school teasing, or other negative comments geared toward him.

Not long ago, a client named Anna called me for a feng shui consult on her home. She stated right up front that her husband had cheated with another woman, and had left her and their two children. When I eventually met her and her youngest child, a son aged five, he seemed to be a little "mini-me" of the father. His words and actions were disrespectful and violent toward his mother. This appeared to be learned behavior from the father. What made this situation worse was that the family dynamic was torn apart by the father leaving and the continuous arguments and confrontations that followed.

Part of my feng shui consultation is making sure the occupants in the home are healthy in body, mind, and spirit. And in this situation, "healthy" was not applicable to the energy of this little boy (or *any* of the home's occupants, really). Emotionally this boy was distraught and angry, and due to his behavior he had been thrown out of three different preschools. Physically, he had a severe case of hives, allergy-asthma symptoms, and a problem with his auditory system. Anna asked me what she could do to help him through this, saying that it was killing her to watch her son be so angry and unbalanced.

Regarding his physical ailments, I devised a plan to conquer and help stabilize his physical symptoms. I recommended soft healing music to play at night before bed or in the car to help both his auditory system and his anger. I suggested she place him in a child yoga class, that he receive magnetic acupuncture treatments, and that he get a nightly massage from her, along with positive affirmations and positive reassurance, all to help him become more balanced.

As for his reoccurring hives and asthma-allergy symptoms, I explained to her that these were from his fear, stemming from his father's attitudes and behavior and from the feelings of being unwanted or not being cherished in this world. She acknowledged that the father did not want this child from the beginning. In fact, he told her this many times throughout her pregnancy. She also said that even though the boy looked and acted just like the father (they also have the same astrological sign and numerology life-path number, which I found very interesting), the father conveyed to his child that he was not wanted.

It quickly became clear to me that in order to dissipate these symptoms, as well as any reoccurring illnesses, it would take both action and unconditional love on Anna's part. And the first action would have to be recognizing the parent-child reflections in relation to these symptoms. Then, and only then, would she be able to make proper use of alternative healing therapies, including alternative expressive outlets that were healthy for this little boy to release and help deal with his emotions.

Child Affirmations

Just like with adult affirmations, which are discussed in detail in Chapter 14, child affirmations are to be used over and over. Parents need to remind their children to practice them, type and hand-write them, say them and hear them. For example, you can say to your child, "You are perfect. I could not have wished for a more perfect child." You can come up with your own phrasing, of course, but be sure to emphasize perfection.

You can even post affirmation notes around your home. It might also be very beneficial to pick an issue that you recognize is a problem for your child. For example, my daughter's curly hair can become quite frizzy, and is never shiningly straight, but it *is* very beautiful. I posted a note on her bathroom mirror: "You have the most beautiful curly hair in all the world!"

Even if your children are in their teens, positive affirmations can help build their self-esteem and self-confidence.

Sense of Belonging

I often refer to my children as my little lions: TayTay Lion, Frankie Lion, and Steven Lion. I call their daddy Daddy Lion, and I am Mommy Lion. Then there is Grandma Lion, our dog Lou-Lou Lion, and so forth. Doing this helps to create a sense of belonging to the family group. There is a tender yet majestic beauty in a lion family . . . in the forming of a pride, where they lick each other's faces and rub heads and cheeks together, exuding a sense of protection, belonging, and love. Theirs is a clear demonstration of a family bonding experience. Offer this love to your own children, and teach them compassion by example. Make a space for them to feel nurtured and enveloped by a sure sense of belonging.

Death and Dying

As covered earlier, it's important for you to create healthy outlets for your child's emotions, especially with events pertaining to death and dying. Their fears can manifest as anger, sadness, denial, guilt, etc. Let them express these emotions in a way that is natural for them. In this way, you will contribute to a constructive and healing space for them.

When my mother passed in September of 2006, my daughter had just turned nine. As I went into her bedroom to help her put on her dress and stockings for the funeral, I noticed that her whiteboard was on the floor. Taylor had drawn a little girl with curly hair and tears coming down to the ground. She had written above it, "I miss you, Grandma." The picture had other things in it, too, like a golden cross, and some clouds in the sky. The whole picture's contents indicated to me that she was expressing her sadness through the art. I knew then, at that moment, to give her creative outlets for her feelings, as discussed earlier in this chapter.

I explained to her that it is healthy and important to express her feelings through art and/or the written word. I also explained that she should write all the funny and good moments between her and her grandma so that she would have these memories forever, even when she starts to forget. We got a journal specifically for Grandma, and Taylor wrote in it for the several months following her death.

I suggest that you find a healthy outlet of expression that suits your child and the event that she is going through. This can be a truly therapeutic way of dealing with difficult emotions that may be hard to understand, regardless of the age of the child.

Healing Your Child

I believe that you can heal your children, both emotionally and during physical illness. Here are some techniques and tips for doing so.

> *Breathwork*—This is essential for destressing, and has a detoxifying, calming effect. For example while a child is brushing his teeth, instruct him to take long, deep breaths that fill the lungs; then, after a few minutes of this, have him stick out his tongue and pant like a dog: quick pants. This revitalizes the lungs and your child.

> *Talk and listen*—At the first sign of sore throat, consider the possible cause—anger or a feeling of not being able to speak up for oneself or to express feelings. (And remember: the child could be reflecting a parent's anger, and often the sore throat is accompanied by a fever, which is often an expression of unresolved anger.) Take time out with your child; lie down and talk with him at night, and just listen. You might be surprised at what your child will say.

> *Archetypal Reiki*—Reiki is a healing system that entails laying of the hands on or above a person's body for the purpose of healing and energy

exchange. This is a technique that children really enjoy, and any parent can do it. Have the child sit up; find the point beside each shoulder blade, in the bony hollow area. Massage each side in clockwise circles for a few moments. Then make a loose fist and lightly tap the child's chest eighteen to twenty times. This technique stimulates the immune system and the heart chakra. Also, gently touch and massage around the child's neck, up and around the ears and lower face; this will open up the throat chakra and help release toxins from the lymph. The child will love the attention and will feel very special, and this energy and love exchange will facilitate healing.

Food and drink intake—Eliminate fruit juices and sodas loaded with sugar; instead, encourage your child to drink water. This is a great way to keep one's glycemic level stable throughout the day, and your child will feel hydrated and energized. And remember, healthy whole foods equal a healthy whole body. Also look into getting a juicer. Juicing greens and beets with apple and carrot is a terrific way to keep your child's "engine" running clean. (Store-bought juice tends to be high in sugar, pasteurized or processed, and does not have the same great health benefits.) You'll also notice an improvement in behavior and a more positive attitude. Start with little shot glasses for the juice, and cheer on your child to make it fun.

Skin brushing—In addition to adequate hydration, skin brushing is awesome for the skin. Skin brushing releases toxins from lymph. Skin brushes are sold at most health-food stores and at bed-and-bath stores. Skin brushing is great for children, but also for us moms and dads, too (an added benefit: it breaks up and smooths out cellulite). Always brush gently toward your heart. The best time for skin brushing is right before a shower or bath, because the dead skin cells coming off will be easily washed down the drain.

Creating a Physical Environment That Fosters Success

The basic concept of feng shui, which you'll learn all about in Chapter 10, is to work with the natural flow of energy. Creating or enhancing positive energy will uplift and support not only *your* environment, but your child's environment, as well. For any kind of studies your child does, her personal space is important to evaluate. Let's look at some good practices for children.

Make sure that before your child has major school requirements like (SAT, final exams, entrance exams, first-grade spelling tests, etc.), you really look at what is in your child's room, as far as clutter and disorganization. Just as important are the garage and/or basement of your home. Yes, having the home clear of clutter can dramatically improve your child's test scores. If you can clear out and clean up your home, your child will likely feel a conscious shift of positive energy. Their home is their "home base." If they can feel strong, organized, safe, and nurtured, you're sure to witness a "home run." Start with the following easy-to-do tips:

Assess *your child's room*—Anything in a child's energy space affects the quality of his sleep, so clear out what's under his bed and give that space a nice vacuuming.

As for drawers and dressers, make sure you go through old clothes and declutter anything that the child has outgrown and/or does not like. Also declutter any toys, books, and supplies that are no longer in use.

Practice aromatherapy—Children love to smell good things, and will really enjoy various aromatherapies. Aromatherapy is great feng shui. In feng shui, aromatherapy serves to bring the energy, or chi, of the body into balance and a state of healing, as well as promotes mental clarity through the sense of smell. My favorite aromatherapy for children is vanilla, as it opens the heart chakra to love and stimulates both energy and mental powers. (Aromatherapy is discussed in more detail in Chapter 13, "The Gift of Healing.")

Leave notes—Children love receiving notes. Notes of love, notes offering encouragement, notes of reassurance, and notes relating to beauty and self-confidence are all a way to inspire your child to believe in themselves, to have the courage and self-confidence to be able to function in today's world, and to feel beautiful.

Praise and encouragement will feed your child's soul and fill the pangs of emotional, spiritual and physical hunger.

Teach your child about beauty, strength, love and goodness, and you will set him on a path toward empowerment and an abundant life.

Remember not only for your child, but also for all of the children who come before you in this life, that where there is love, there is God. God is within our hearts. And with God, all things are possible.

⤐ 7 ⤏

The Gift of Darkness

We must know and come to accept the fact that although we contain Spirit and are spiritual beings, we are, of course, human. All of life consists of cycles: the lives of all animals revolve around cycles, as do the moon and the stars, the oceans, the forests, and even the seasons. We, too, as humans, have cycles on all levels: physical, emotional, and spiritual. Our physical bodies—most notably those of women; just look at menses cycles and menopause—go through changes and cycles. These same cycles pertain to our emotional and spiritual sense of self. We have times of light, joy, happiness, and confidence, as well as darkness, gloom, sadness, and doubt. It's inescapable: there are both ups and downs, crests and troughs, in everyone's lives. The challenge is to accept that, lean into it, and be thankful for it. We cannot ignore our physical nature—and the necessity of experiencing both darkness and light—by trying to be some kind of "perfect" spiritual being. Doing that will only create judgment and conflict within us.

Often people hold unrealistic beliefs or attitudes about their limitations or shortcomings. Sometimes—okay, a lot of times—I work until I overdo it and come near complete exhaustion. The truth is, I'm constantly trying to balance each day: meditating/praying, working, fitting in yoga or an hour on the treadmill, meeting book deadlines, washing school uniforms, spending time with the children, dating, seeing friends, cooking, cleaning . . . the list goes on. And I admit I hold myself to a tough schedule and I push myself every day to do more and to do it more perfectly. When I *do* exhaust myself, whether physically or emotionally, or both, I say to myself, "Tina, you shouldn't be sick, run-down, or depressed today; you're supposed to be a perfect spiritual counselor, the 'feng shui lady,' a self-help author, Superwoman!" The end result is that I feel embarrassed and guilty for having run myself down. But these thoughts are self-sabotaging and create undue stress and self-loathing.

We must choose self-love at every moment to create a balance between the dark and the light within us. Guilt is the biggest emotion that accompanies one's darkness. Release this now, give yourself a break, and love who you are *now*. Accept the darkness, and the fear that comes with it. Savor each moment of this darkness: the grief, the depression and the despair—really experience the depths of your feelings, own them, and then let the darkness go. In this way, you can begin to live more positively and be lighter in heart, mind, and soul.

Know that when you are feeling shadowed by some emotion, when you are feeling darkness within or around you, it is simply one of the low moments (or one of the "low energy" periods) in your life. That's all. Know that you are worthy and on your way back up . . . to wholeness, to the brilliant ascent of enlightenment. When you are *really* at the bottom, know that very little else, if anything, can go wrong. It may feel like it's the worst, like your very existence could melt away into the earth and dissipate into nothingness. But every moment that passes while you are at the bottom moves you closer to your own divine place of self-realization and empowerment. By opening your eyes in the darkness, you will discover your true convictions, and you'll find the courage to stay true to them.

When you travel through darkness, there is nowhere to go but toward the light. Even though the outcome may not be clear and the reasoning may not be apparent, you still have embarked on the path toward enlightenment. You have already embarked on your path (through the choices you've made), and you must keep going. Darkness and destruction are necessary for spiritual enlightenment. Anything you do to try to stop it, stall it, or resist it will only bring you increased pain and possibly despair. If you feel like you are going through a very dark place, fear not—something new is struggling to be born. And with this birth come rebirth, light, and renewal of the self.

When we look at the purely physical world surrounding depression, we see the following: you cry, you experience great fatigue, you feel lonely, gloomy, perhaps even desperate . . . you feel "depressed." If this goes on longer than two weeks, we are told by today's medical establishment (and society in general) that we are suffering from a disease called "clinical depression." We are then encouraged to try some pharmaceutical medication. As a nurse for many years, I have seen the comings and goings of various antidepressant and anti-anxiety medicines. These medications come from huge conglomerate drug companies that are being fully supported by the government and, in turn, the drug companies give the prescribing physicians rewards for dispensing the drugs.

Regardless of whether you believe these drugs contaminate your body or help your body, one thing is certain: they provide you, your body, and your mind with a mask, and in so doing, they detach you, sometimes subtly and sometimes not so subtly, from your truth. I am not declaring that all prescription depression medications are horrible and we mustn't take them. Indeed, there are instances in which such medication is a much-needed part of a patient's care plan and is very beneficial to the welfare of the patient. My intention in raising this matter is solely to spark your intuition about the "why" of a person's depression and to offer a garbage can—make that a red biohazard bag—in which to dump the feelings of guilt and fear that so often come along with depression or any other psychological-emotional "disease."

I know two things to be true: First, if you *do* have depression, you are in a state of darkness. I like to call it the Gift of Darkness. Second, the darkness is *real*. I believe it's human and normal to feel great, awake, happy, energized, optimistic, and positive . . . and then have moments in which you feel isolated, run-down, alone, sad, and depressed. Some purely spiritual self-help gurus state that depression is not real, but rather an illusion—we just *think* the depression is real. However, I've observed that if we hold this to be true, we feel even *more* guilty for feeling depressed. There is such an incredible amount of guilt we place on ourselves, both consciously and subconsciously, for feeling depression. Through it all, one question remains: How do we get out of this state called depression?

Let's say you're in a room with absolutely no light and no windows—it's complete darkness. Do you really want medication to cloud you and make you feel stagnant—physically, emotionally, and spiritually? Do you really want to get numb and disconnect from your true feelings, your "emotions of darkness"? Yes, medication will help you calm down and perhaps focus better, but you'll still be in this pitch-dark room for what could be an awfully long time, focusing on . . . what?

When you mask yourself with medication, no true depression, no true anxiety, no true introspection about your fears, no real contemplation about your inner obstacles, can ever take place. So ask yourself, *Why do I want to just sit in the dark feeling numb?* What about asking, *Why am I in this dark room? And how did I get here? What is the purpose of this darkness?*

Sooner or later, guess what happens (and has happened to thousands who've tried this approach)? You eventually find your way back to "light" . . . either by feeling around for the light switch or by finding the doorknob to open the door, bringing light and freedom. It sounds like a silly analogy, but it is that simple. If we can understand what is happening, we can help ourselves and start leading a richer and happier life. Drugs (both prescription and illicit) are used to alter consciousness—period.

When you find yourself in that dark room, take in all the emotions that come with it. Feel these emotions and really own them. Take responsibility for them. Again, really savor what is happening; because when you pass through the darkness to the light, you will discover that you are holding aloft the flaming torch, the power of light, in your own hand. You will see that you have become stronger than you ever were before. And when the darkness passes, you will begin to understand the "why" of the darkness more clearly, and to recognize the pieces of your life falling more perfectly into place.

So, what is the answer?

The first component is self-love. Are you taking care of your physical body through good nutrition, adequate rest, exercise, yoga, massage, meditation, journaling, and/or prayer? Taking care of our physical body has the most impact on our emotional state, whether we want to admit it or not. To truly balance mind, body, and spirit, we must take a close look at how we actively *care* for all of these things and incorporate self-care (i.e., self-love) into our daily routine.

Another component is to turn to your support system: Do you have someone to look to for guidance in your life? Someone to talk to for support? Your faith can also serve as a support system. Having faith that you will be guided and supported through any darkness is essential. You may feel as though the cups of your heart, the cups of your life, have all spilled. If so, you must acknowledge—*know now*—that these cups will be filled with new life. The darkness *and* the light that you have experienced in your life have led you to this very moment. Right here, this moment becomes the road to your future—to your healing, balance, and peace. This entails having a complete faith . . . enough faith to let go, to let everything fall into Spirit's/God's hands of Grace, knowing that everything will be "okay."

The third component of the answer is to go inward and contemplate. Take time for introspection, allowing room for healing to take place. This will allow your higher consciousness, your Spirit-guided consciousness, to plant seeds . . . and, in time, the seeds will sprout a new understanding and clarity.

Whenever I think of withdrawing from worldly considerations, I think of the Hermit card in a tarot deck, which represents the familiar archetype of the Wise One who emerges from a deep, dark place. The Hermit is a old wise man or woman—holding a lantern. That old person symbolizes the wisdom of age and a state of maturity. The flame of the lantern is a symbol of clarity—the lantern is your light, given to you to illuminate your path and send more light into the world.

Sometimes Spirit wants us to pause, to reflect, to contemplate on how to best "divvy up our doings" and to assess ourselves. It means, essentially, withdrawing from the outer world to look deep within the self. The Hermit shows that this is the time when you need to be alone in order to look deep within for answers. Finding time for this break for introspection is very important. Taking a vacation, long or short—a plane ride or a boat ride or a nice drive down the highway—can be eye-opening "Hermit time." But if you can't escape your responsibilities or don't have financial means right away for such an excursion, it can be just as efficient to merely set aside time each day to meditate, read something inspirational, journal, contemplate and/or pray.

Becoming aware of your true self and working through the emotions of darkness will allow you to come into light. Then you can radiate that light back out into the world that you just withdrew from. Above all, I believe the lesson of the Hermit shows us that *inside* ourselves we carry the light and love that we have too often sought *outside* of ourselves. Given the proper attitude, the mystery of solitude and the dawning of self-realization are like the unwrapping of the *Gift of Darkness* . . . with a sense of wonderment about what might be inside. Be patient and kind toward yourself. By searching your inner sanctum for truth, you will become more like the wise old Hermit. If you are encountering darkness in your life, take this time and raise up your lamp to illuminate your path.

For every death there will be new birth. For every darkness there will be new light. The veil is that darkness is the end. The mystery is to discover that it is just the beginning.

⇐ 8 ⇒

The Gift of the Star

In every tarot deck, there is a Star card that signifies peace, hope, and the realization of being One among the One. People must follow their stars to know their truth. We all have the ability to make our dreams come true if we can be who we truly are, and trust our intuition, all the while remaining true to our convictions.

Even amidst the darkest of times, a star is always shining somewhere in the heavens. After one experiences her own personal darkness filled with sadness, fear, anxiety, and depression, and once the light of hope, understanding, and peace begins to return, one's future begins to appear more promising. In numerous ancient spiritual traditions (including the Vedas from India and the tarot from the Middle East), the star offers insights into our journey toward spiritual realization. It offers us a guiding light, a clear direction, and a source of vibrant energy.

I love hearing the phrase, "It's written in the stars," because it indicates that there's something bigger than me and my earthly understanding at play, something divine that gives me a feeling of peace and certainty along with underlying feelings of reassurance and belonging. If and when you go through a "dark night of the soul," look for the shining star in your darkened sky. Start by taking a "time out"—whatever time you require to break free of what has preoccupied your thoughts and emotions. Use that time-out to begin to identify and follow your star, even if only for a moment, or an hour, or a day, or a weekend (if possible, take a week!). Give yourself permission to fully engage in this time-out. Notice the feelings that come forth. You may experience feelings of passion, release, true bliss, high-energy optimism, and undoubting trust. Or you may experience much subtler feelings. What matters is that you are being true to what you're feeling, not stifling anything at all; you're allowing yourself to simply be with and accept your life experience, just as it is. In times of darkness, accompanied by challenging emotions, it's important that you allow yourself to be simple and innocent, without judgment. This will allow the starshine to emerge more readily in your awareness.

This simple state is the connection to your desires— a bridge to greater self-knowledge; and this eventually leads to the manifestation of that which you truly desire. The simple, natural illumination of your feelings is the first step to success and abundance on all levels: spiritual, material, and emotional. You must pay close attention to these feelings because they mark a doorway of shining light. As you stand at this doorway, the light illuminates your thoughts and intentions; and as you look up to the sky, you will see your star.

I am but a bright star in the galaxy of stars. Knowing and following my star has led me here, to this very page. And when I look up to the stars, I see my part in the grand scheme of this lifetime . . . and my niche in this vast universe. I draw wisdom from this simple knowing, and I more deeply understand my true nature when I meditate upon my star.

In September 2007, I took a weekend trip to Las Vegas. One of my closest girlfriends, Heidi, had invited me to come, all-inclusive. It was a "girls' weekend" and there were four of us on the trip. I knew it would be a perfect opportunity to take a fully deserved time-out—a whole weekend away from my day-to-day reality.

When I left Tampa that day, the plane flew up through the sunset. The sunset was so beautiful when viewed from the ascending plane, and it swept my breath away. The sun cast delicious silky apricot hues, honey yellows, and the light reflections off the thick, puffy clouds were brilliant. I was a witness to God's universal perfection at that very moment. The fading heavenly blues that slowly transcended into indigo black, becoming the night sky, were like a beautiful backdrop for the entire starry cosmos. Gratitude and awe filled me. I felt deeply blessed, like I was being sprinkled with fairy dust that enraptured my heart with lightness. I knew, at that moment, a new state of freedom. Certainly, I felt, these were a few stolen moments of God's Grace, while I sat amidst 200 passengers on a Southwest 747.

When the plane touched the tarmac in Las Vegas, I still carried this awe-inspired sense of divinity. I felt a sort of enlightenment as we landed, as the lights around me shone brightly like a thousand stars were joyfully greeting me. The van ride to the hotel, the tall buildings, the bright neon lights, the city-made orchestra of sounds all reminded me of the immense beauty and richness of the stars in the sky. Then there was the hotel suite, with its fancy shower, the delicately fragranced soap, the fresh towels; all of these things were so surprisingly and utterly amazing—and rejuvenating—to me.

The next day, awakening to the morning light (which is also a "star"), the view of the mountains, my morning coffee—everything moved me in such a way that I could only be taken aback and filled with grace. I knew I was going to get in some fantastic writing on my book—a solid chapter or two coming to fruition. I felt gratitude in every fiber of my being, for each moment . . . and then I became conscious and aware of the importance for me to continue this feeling, to savor this feeling, this grace and gratitude, through the whole trip. Leave it to me, Tina Coluccio, to find rainbows and butterflies in a city known for sex, drugs, partying, and gambling. Somehow I did.

Justin Timberlake was performing that weekend and he was staying at the same hotel, just a few floors above us. We spent the two days in the Moorea Beach Club private poolside area while Mr. Timberlake was a few stairs away in a more private section.

There were more "star" experiences to be had on this trip. The guys from the Grammy Award–winning rock band Linkin Park hung out with us for a few hours by the pool. Then there were the front-row tickets to see Justin Timberlake later that night. But the point of all this was not that I was overwhelmingly "star-struck"; rather, it was that all of these experiences seemed to be laid out before me, and I was more excited about being in my awestruck state of grace. Yes, my ego enjoyed the fancy hotel, the unlimited food and drink, the "coolness" of being on "the list" to get into the private poolside, etc. This was a once-in-a-lifetime experience for me (as it would be for so many), and I truly enjoyed the royal treatment. And I made sure to be conscious of it while enjoying it. And yet the spiritual realization and "grace" status felt *so much more tangible*, so much more meaningful and fulfilling.

In that state, I felt in total connection with God, with Universal Will, with Universal Truth. It brought on a quiet, spiritually centered, complete euphoria. Living in a state of grace, I believe, offers much more fulfillment than a celebrity life or being wealthy . . . and it is available to all of us, no matter what our social or economic status.

My pen was set to the page for the duration of the plane ride back to Tampa. My friend Nicole, with whom I'd spent the majority of my time in Vegas, wore a diamond pendant in the shape of a big star during the entire trip. Her diamond star seemed to twinkle, drawing my attention as if to trigger a message from Spirit, and a creative stirring. And so, like a miracle birth, this chapter, "The Gift of the Star," was born!

This "star-filled" weekend really amounted to me getting a new grasp on my own reality. I set upon the weekend as a way to engage myself in some much-needed self-analysis and prioritizing, kind of like taking a break to assess exactly where I was in the scheme of my life . . . to make sure I moved forward into the future with my needs and my passion front and center. I asked myself, *What is my truth? Have I been living my truth? Am I staying congruent with my personal goals, those relating to what I feel passionate about and conviction of purpose?* There was *something* that I needed to clarify. And that *something* turned out to be the *truth, my truth* . . . the Light that guides me . . . *the truth of my "star."*

I contemplated all of my titles in life: the mother, the homemaker, and the wife, of course. But in addition to those, I contemplated my professional occupation: I contemplated why I went to college for nursing fresh out of high school. I contemplated why I was holding a current nursing license, still working a few months out of the year in nursing. I thought about my training as a feng shui consultant. I contemplated doing intuitive counseling and spiritual-reading sessions. I even contemplated a title that I had never considered for myself: "medical intuitive," which combined the titles of nurse and intuitive counselor.

As I continued pondering my roles and labels, it was like I was flying across the globe on a sabbatical to sit, one-on-one, with Buddha. It was as though I'd come to hear Buddha's questioning, so that I might leave a little more enlightened, with a little more self-knowledge. *Am I a nurse? No! Am I a medical intuitive? Nah, not really. Am I an intuitive counselor? I can do it, yes . . . but no, it's not my future. Am I feng shui consultant? Yes, I studied and became a feng shui master, and yes, I lecture and teach on the subject; but it feels like a stepping stone, like it is just one M&M among a handful of them.* Then I got to my last question from Buddha: *Are you a writer? Are you the author of* The Gift of Spirit? *Yes! Yes, I am!*

All of my pondering and wondering about who or what I am had finally—and triumphantly—concluded with a self-evident, self-affirming realization . . . an "I am" experience that was truly magnificent! Immediately, a feeling of peace came over me—a peace that, with a soft, graceful whisper, said, This is who I am. This is my contribution to the world. This is my gift . . . and I absolutely love it! I can breathe freely, joyfully, and knowingly! For me, it's amazing, each day, to come to the page and write. I feel connected, I feel bliss, and I feel it's the whole bag of M&Ms, not just one!

When I stepped off of the plane back home in Tampa, I knew with undying confidence that other than a writer, I *can't* be anything else. It feels like I have no choice and there's not one reason to deny myself my truth, my calling, one moment longer. Even to this day, I have absolutely no idea how much money I might make as a writer or how much income can be had from publishing this book, and honestly it makes no difference. I would do this for free, because I feel so full and I have connected with so many of my gifts, and to that there is no monetary comparison. I've been blessed with not only the Gift of Spirit, but also with knowing the passions of my heart and knowing my great purpose here on earth. To know and feel this every day of my life is priceless. I feel so blessed by the fullness that comes from being in touch with Spirit.

I am ever so grateful to come to the realization that the sum of my previous titles and the sum of all of these experiences is the discovery of my life purpose. I have felt each title to be of great value, like a set of stones upon which I have had the privilege to set my foot in order to walk on life's journey. The sum of your titles and your experiences generates your own unique "star," but it is your passion and life purpose that makes it shine so bright and twinkle in the night sky.

To find your star, meditate on what you truly desire. Connect with your heart and ask yourself, *What is it that will make me truly happy? What do I truly desire? What is my passion?* Meditate on this until you know *your* truth. Contemplate your titles. Pursue a vision of yourself beyond all previous titles. A great change is in the making: a revelation of your creative powers, and a gift of deep self-knowledge. It is simply for you to ask Spirit for guidance to see into your own heart and soul . . . to find—and then follow—your own shining star.

~

My path has not always been easy. Over and over, I have watched the wreckage pile up from what I assumed to be the best direction for me to find and live the highest truth and the truest happiness. Everything I knew has, at one time or another, slipped out of my hands . . . and only one thing has remained constant: change. Everything else falls away. I had to learn to move steadily in the way of love, both giving love and receiving love.

Your faith, your dreams, and your future are in the stars. Focus on this. Through the Divine Star that shines within the most sacred aspect of each of us comes forth a message that declares, *Spirit shines through all things.* Just like a star in the cosmos, our role in the universe is one part of a divine magnificent display: the Sacred Circle of Life.

Visualize the stars in a clear night sky. The star you see is a happy message from spirit saying, "it's all good." Let the stars be inspiring, stay optimistic, and stay positive. Think of the star of Bethlehem, which heralded new life.

At this moment, your future is bright; your star is rising. You have found the beginning of your truth and have set foot upon your path toward empowerment. All that is material will eventually die; everything you know to be your reality will be stripped away for a chance at the stars of discovery and enlightenment. All that will be left is your spirit. *Your spirit, your star, is there . . . it is there with mine.*

❧ 9 ❧

The Gift of Resurrection

When I think of "resurrection" just before Easter each year, I immediately sense around me a swirling, revealing, life-giving energy—the energy of spiritual resurrection! The timing of this sensation makes perfect sense, as we approach Easter time each year, the holiday in which millions of people around the world celebrate the resurrection of Jesus (or, as some say, the Christ). Regardless of your chosen religion and whether or not we call it "spiritual rebirth" or "spiritual renewal" or "resurrection," the core meaning is the same: *a path of return.* It is a return to God, a return to the One.

You might say, "Yes, Tina, that's great and all, but how does that pertain to my reality?" And the answer is that it starts with self-review and a mindful return to consciously walking your path. Ask yourself these questions:

- How do you really feel about yourself at this moment in time?

- Have you done the best you could?

- Has your thinking been positive?

- Have your actions supported that positivity?

- Have you devoted yourself to your work and to humanity as a whole in a positive way?

- Are you living with passion and purpose?

- Are you moving forward with goodness?

- Are you full of judgment or anger toward others?

- Has your heart become light?

- Do you love both giving and receiving *without strings*?

Journal these answers for yourself, and take time to reflect on your responses.

Take some time to really look at where you are at this moment; take some time for a brief "self review" . . . but with a mind to let go of judgment toward yourself and others. Judgment of others has no meaning; it only fills you with negativity. Carrying around judgment of others is worse for your heart than eating saturated fats! When you accept others the way they are, holding no expectations of them, this gives you an endearing quality that draws goodness and light to you.

Re-examine your answer to the question, *Who am I?* Our lives are in a process of continual re-creation, based upon our thoughts and our actions, and at this time—right now—a big change, a powerful transformation of world and individual consciousness, is underway! Every thought can radiate outward in the brilliance of divine love and divine light. And from here on out, every good thing that happens to you will be very well deserved.

We are being called to a more meaningful way of life: a rebirth of wisdom and of our spiritual selves. Many of us have reached the lowest point on the cycle of life, and have come to know firsthand the difficult emotions of fear and pain, grief and loss; and we are now ready to move onward, to come to terms with life in all its glory! We are ready to be reborn—to begin afresh. We are ready to be resurrected and reborn into new thinking, into a completely new stage of consciousness. We are entering a new cycle in the grand scheme of life!

Through our development of more keen spiritual insight and recognition, our false illusions—our false truths—will fall by the wayside. Through redemption and resurrection, our old ways of thinking and of being will be destroyed. This will be a *natural* destruction, a positive form of purging. We do not have to fear this type of destruction, for it is in the context of creating something new (and better) from that which no longer serves our highest good. When this phase of our spiritual evolution is complete, we will be awakened by the "white light" of universal consciousness and universal truth.

Be resurrected in light, and begin to remake your universe, living each moment in the image of love and light.

Part III

Fulfilling Your Destiny—Attaining Peace, Love, and Happiness

⋐ 10 ⋑

The Gift of Feng Shui

Feng shui, in a nutshell, is the art of balancing, harmonizing, and enhancing the flow of natural energy. It is an ancient Chinese system of aesthetics believed to utilize the laws of both heaven (astronomy) and earth (geography) to help one improve one's life by increasing the flow of positive chi (life force or energy, often spelled "qi") into one's environment and self. Essentially, it is about living consciously on this earth, becoming truly aware of your surroundings, and enjoying and really living the highest quality of life possible. I view feng shui as a great way of opening one's awareness from the ground up. I am passionate about feng shui, and I always have fun when incorporating it into my own home or workplace. I also encourage each client to have fun, using "lightness" as an underlying palette when approaching the tastes and traditions of feng shui.

Feng shui can be used by all people, from all walks of life, all ages, all religious backgrounds, and in all countries around the world. Sometimes people shun the very thought of feng shui because they simply don't understand it or because they assume it will go against a religious belief. But feng shui is not a religion. It is simply the art of having awareness about what is going on around you. It can only *complement* your religion and *empower* your beliefs.

The underlying principle in feng shui is that everything is made of chi. Feng shui's principles and enhancements are based on using our surroundings to help direct good chi into our homes and businesses, thereby increasing the peace, harmony, balance, and success in our lives.

We have all walked into someone's home and immediately felt uneasy, a "something's not right" or "creepy" vibe. Well, if you're feeling this, you're likely sensing that the chi of the home is not positive. It is as though the elements of the home do not combine to make an "auspicious" environment. But something can *always* be done to improve the situation, and that's where feng shui comes into play!

I love the line "Just the two of us building castles in the sky" from the Bill Withers song "Just the Two of Us": Are you living in your castle in the sky—your dream home? Your home, no matter what it costs or where it is, should bring you feelings of comfort and delight—the *ahhh* can and *should* be there. The inside of a home is the inside of a home, whether that home is a three-million-dollar mansion or a double-wide trailer. In my many years of doing feng shui consultations, I have learned one cardinal rule: before proceeding, one ought to be conscious of and accepting of the living space you are in at that very moment. Life is too short to not move beyond the ego to recognize and appreciate where you are living right now. Stop *dreaming* of your dream home—start living in it *today*.

One of my first clients as a feng shui consultant was a little old lady (around 80+ years of age) who had come to a health expo in Clearwater Beach, Florida, at which I had a feng shui booth set up with different crystals, bamboo, and my consultation literature. This elderly woman, looking a bit sad and moving slowly, migrated over to my booth. She asked about feng shui, and after I explained it in great length, she wondered if I'd be willing to go to her home, which happened to be a trailer.

Arriving at her trailer that following Saturday, I was struck with both a bolt of compassion and a jolt of eagerness to help feng shui her small home and clear out her space. As I began looking around, surveying the space she'd been dwelling in for years, I came to understand why she'd looked so sad and seemed so lonely upon my first meeting her. As we went through the feng shui of her home, I explained the different life stations, and pointed out and cleared a lot of the clutter that was present. And immediately, she started breathing better and smiling more. I then saw in her eyes a total release from the cluttered and constricted energy that had burdened her, as though a great weight had been lifted off of her shoulders. She said she finally felt safe, at peace, and free. She also said that she could now live out the rest of her days there with joy. She died a few years later, and I felt blessed to have been of service to her for her final years of peaceful life.

My first business consultation came when I was teaching an introductory class on feng shui at a bookstore, and a lady dressed in business attire came up to me after the talk. She said she was the new CEO of a national telecommunications company based in Tampa, and would like me to do a business consultation. She was taking over as CEO because the company was ranked last in the country for customer service and sales. We set up a feng shui consult that following Saturday.

When I arrived, we went over the feng shui of the building and the structural design of the offices versus the cubicles. I explained that the basic cubicle is not in a "commanding" position, which makes one feel like there is someone always looking over your shoulder . . . and *that* can negatively affect your mindset and work productivity on a subconscious level. I ordered 300 small round mirrors that went on every computer monitor so that each employee would feel in a more commanding position while sitting in the cubicles. We brought in a sizable number of small trees throughout the office and small flowering plants in the break rooms. Among other things, I had the CEO start each morning by calling in positive chi through intention and prayer. I had her focus on the feeling of abundance and flowing positive chi derived from the huge fountain that was located in the front of the building. With this being my first business consultation, I was eager to see the results. She called me a few months later and said, "Tina, you're not going to believe this: the staff productivity and the harmony between everyone has *significantly* improved! It's been three months and we are now third in the country in terms of staff productivity. From last, to third . . . in the country!"

What I would like most for people to get out of feng shui is a link between spiritual well-being and both personal and business growth. In one's career, proper feng shui can be a vital element of a successful business. Who wouldn't want to enhance business prospects and increase profits? Some of the most wealthy and successful people and businesses use feng shui. Rita Wilson, Madonna, and Kimora Lee Simmons have all employed it, as has Donald

Trump. Trump has a golden globe in front of one of his Trump Towers, sitting in protection of his building, warding off any negative energy—just one of many feng shui enhancements that he has implemented. The following companies are among the many that have also used feng shui: McDonald's, Chase Manhattan Bank, Lockheed Martin, Coca-Cola's US division, Procter & Gamble, and *InStyle* magazine.

By being aware of the space around you and the *energy* in the space around you, you can create a *sacred balance* in your life. There are two aspects to this sacred balance: The *sacred* part is what I consider to be the spiritual part of feng shui, and it entails the intention you hold, your intuition, and the practice of meditation and prayer. The *balance* part is the answer to the question, *What is physically surrounding you that is creating your environment?* This pertains to things like furniture, plants and landscaping, toilets, plumbing, paint color, flooring, stairs, etc.

With proper use of feng shui, you can improve your health, create harmony in your relationships, increase your wealth, and create a happier home and workplace . . . in other words, more and more abundance on all levels. How superb is that?

As a feng shui master consultant, I service my clients' homes to benefit their personal energy and the energy of their surroundings, much in the way a financial planner makes the most of what a client already has and hopefully sets up the client for the future. The financial planner has been trained to work with money, has studied the market and the economy, and attempts to meet clients' specific goals to make them feel financially safe and secure. I "feel" the energy of a space and have experience in reading what's going on inside of you (energetically) and around your space. I can, therefore, suggest changes and focus in on enhancements that will help manifest more positive energy, which can greatly impact and positively influence your life.

The same principles that exist for your body are true for your surroundings. The food and drink you consume ultimately affect your body, which can feel full, content, calm, healthy, clean, buoyant, elated, and "light" . . . *or* it can feel empty, unsatisfied, anxious, unhealthy/sick, dirty, tired, unhappy, and burdened by excess weight. What we tend not to realize is that our home, our "sacred space," can feel these ways, too. A space can feel burdened by excess weight in the form of negative energy, disorganization, and too much stuff.

This brings us to the subject of clutter. I believe clutter is the number one precursor to what I call "Bad Feng Shui Disease"—so much so that I have dedicated a whole chapter to the subject of clutter. Clutter should, I believe, be singled out and conquered. But we'll tackle clutter in the next chapter, "The Gift of Clutter."

Hopefully you now have a basic understanding of what feng shui is. My hope is that by discovering and implementing good feng shui, you can come to live in a place of peace and harmony. (For more detailed information about feng shui, please consult this book's appendix.)

Every home across all of the countries around the world reaches up to the sky—your home is your castle in the sky. Your castle, my castle . . . we are all in this place together. Look up to heaven in gratitude and feel this connection, then focus on enhancing your life and fortune, thereby contributing to the greater good of mankind and the world. Becoming aware and having good feng shui make a positive difference in your life and the lives of your loved ones. Prosperity, joy, peace, love, generosity, growth, knowledge, expansion, spirituality, and soul growth are the most significant and wondrous experiences of this lifetime . . . and feng shui can help enhance all of them.

Feng shui is an art . . . and it is painted on a canvas upon which your passions, philosophy, religion, design, and culture come together to become a beautiful masterpiece.

≈ 11 ≈

The Gift of Clutter

Clutter is often defined as having too many things in a designated space; things that are untidy, messy, or disorganized; anything unfinished, broken and/or not of use; and things you no longer value or love. However, there are other, more subtle aspects to "clutter."

Clutter of any kind causes stagnant energy and affects you physically, mentally, emotionally, and spiritually. To simply recognize and remove your clutter will transform your life by: 1) releasing negative, stagnant energy; 2) creating space for magnificent things to come in; and 3) generating positive energy. Clutter is one of the main killers of your chi, just as heart disease is one of the major killers of your physical body.

You already know that feng shui is the art of balancing the flow of energy in your surroundings to create peace and harmony. And while incorporating good feng shui is an essential part of living in balance, it is imperative to understand the link between feng shui and clutter. Karen Kingston wrote a wonderful easy-to-understand book entitled *Clear Your Clutter with Feng Shui*, which, along with her other books, has been a base of knowledge to grow my own practice.

Feng Shui and Clutter

If there is a particular area of your home or workplace that is cluttered, look to see in what area of the Bagua map (see the appendix) it is located, and check to see what is happening in that aspect of your life. For instance, having clutter in the Wealth/Prosperity area can create financial problems in your life. Using a feng shui cure (like a mirror, for example) in this area to generate more wealth can actually double your financial hardship if the area is not clear of clutter.

I have worked with a lot of clients who go headfirst to the Wealth section to set up feng shui cures with a "show me the money" attitude, without realizing or grasping the entire concept of feng shui and clutter. Clutter of any kind creates an obstacle to the flow of energy around a space. This in turn creates a stagnant atmosphere in the lives of the occupants, who eventually begin feeling that stagnancy within themselves. It always starts small, but it grows, bit by bit. This stagnation can lead to internal confusion and chaos, which can eventually be experienced as anxiety, emotional upset, or depression (I've seen this happen in my own life). The bottom line is this: When you're surrounded by clutter, it is impossible to have 100 percent clarity about what you're doing in your life. Clutter inside breeds clutter outside. If you're facing clutter in any area of your life (external or internal), ask yourself this question: *What obstacles or fears are holding me back from moving forward and keeping me from being the person I was meant to be?*

Honing Down to the Essentials

Have you ever felt elated and superexcited about staying in a hotel room or suite? On my last trip, I really thought about it and asked myself why I get so thrilled. I concluded that it's because it has all the essentials *without any clutter.* For example, my last trip was a two-nighter at the Ritz-Carlton in Sarasota, Florida. I was surrounded by fresh, clean sheets; a clean bathroom made of white marble (toilet, shower, and sink); a spectacular TV; a minifridge; a clean, plush leather chair in which to sit; a clean and clear desk on which to write; and a little balcony on which to get fresh air and look out over my surroundings. This feeling is the same feeling I have at my own home after maintaining my declutterment and having the house clean and tidy.

When you get rid of clutter, you will literally feel lighter in body, mind, and spirit. The stagnant energy from clutter can cause tiredness and lethargy. Clutter can keep you in the past, with the result that there is no room for anything new to come into your life. You have to release the past for a better tomorrow, for you to attract all the wonderful things you want in your life.

Using the Bagua can be an excellent way to check which area of your life you have been sabotaging by having clutter in the corresponding area of your home. Give some thought to what you would like to have in each area of your life. Here are some tips to get started:

> *Analyze and sort*—Identify what is important to you, and group similar items. With each item ask yourself, *Why am I holding on to this?* If it does not serve a positive purpose in your life, detach from it and release it.

Purge—Decide what you can get rid of and how to get rid of it (e.g., have a garage sale, make donations, throw things in the garbage).

Designate space—Decide where the "to be saved" items will go, and make it official. As you fill your "purge" bins, move them into a space designated to hold your outgoing items. Be disciplined and strict about these areas.

Organize—Use bins, baskets, and boxes to organize what you save, besides items that are organized in cabinets and closets. Make sure they are good-quality containers, and label them if you cannot see through them. Be creative. For example, having an "incoming mail" basket on top of your desk may be easier and more practical to use than a box or a bin.

Maintain—Spend time each day (as little as five or ten minutes a day can be enough) to maintain what you have done and keep things tidy.

If you are feeling overwhelmed or the job seems insurmountable, follow these tips:

Take it slow. Try one room at a time. Start wherever you feel drawn to start. It doesn't matter if it doesn't make sense; start where you feel you need it most. As soon as you begin to clear out the clutter, you will feel a benefit and begin to build energy to move on to the next space.

Hire a cleaning service, even if it's just to start the process.
Cleaning the bathrooms, toilets, mopping, vacuuming, cleaning windows . . . all of this will start moving energy in the right direction and will help you focus on the decluttering task at hand.

While writing this book, working a full-time job, and being a mother to three children, I decided I needed help decluttering. I hired a lady for about four hours on a Saturday afternoon, and ran ahead of her putting away laundry and clearing paperwork, bills, and excess toys (clutter), while she focused on the cleaning. It worked out perfectly, and I felt much better about the energy around the house. It felt clearer, lighter, and more flowing. Hire other help if you need to, such as a lawn service, carpet cleaners, painters, or handymen.

Maintaining a Clutter-Free Space

Some tips for staying clutter free are:

If you don't absolutely love it, get rid of it. Things you really love will carry high vibration energy and will be uplifting. Don't keep something out of guilt because a certain person gave you the item. Anything like unwanted gifts that you keep or things that need fixing will drain your positive energy rather than energize you.

Create an inbox for bills, to-do items, etc. Treat your home like a business, where appropriate, with specific files for specific interactions. For example, keep a file for recipes, a file for any family pets (visits to the vet, rabies certificate, etc.), a file for each car, a file for each child, a file for the electric company, etc.

Create an "upon-entering altar." This is a place to deposit keys, cell phones, wallets, cash/change, etc.

As it comes, let it go. That is, when clutter comes in, such as new toys, receipts, or junk mail, get it assessed and place it where it is supposed to go. Don't let it start to accumulate.

Dump anything that pins you down to a negative emotion! I had a divorced client who kept her old wedding ring. Every time she would go to the place where she kept it in her closet, she would begin to feel hopeless and become sad. After her consultation, she traded in the ring for a beautiful set of diamond earrings. Remember: if it reminds you of something negative, cut it loose.

Have vibrant, lively plants around your space. This provides good energy and represents growth. Get rid of dead or dried flowers or plants, which carry negative energy.

Don't keep things "just in case." Doing so represents a lack of trust in the present moment and a lack of faith and trust in the future. You create your reality by the thoughts you have, so give up this "just in case" thought pattern. Some examples of this are having three coffee makers, way too many Tupperware containers, or outdated products lurking under your bathroom sink.

Complete or discard unfinished items. Anything unfinished in any realm of your space clutters your psyche and nags at you subconsciously. Examples include fixing a broken drawer or a leaking faucet, making phone calls that need to be made, paying bills that pile up.

With regard to specific areas of your home, keep in mind these bits of advice:

Junk drawer—Choose a small drawer and make sure you have regular clear-outs (e.g., quarterly).

Kitchen—Have a regular, major clear-out of your cupboards and refrigerator. This means chucking out packets of soy sauce from 1998, old bottles of Mylanta, etc. Check expiration dates on medicines, supplements, and any condiment or beverage bottles, and throw away anything outdated. If it's in question, throw it out and make a fresh start.

Bedroom—This, especially, should be clutter-free so that you can rest better and have a personal and romantic retreat for yourself and any "significant other." Therefore, don't place exercise equipment, computers, or other nonbedroom materials in this area. Check what is under the bed and over the bed, and clear out those spaces, too.

Desk—A clear desk will always support clear thinking and a clear mind. Keep only the essentials on your desk: for example, phone, computer, an "inbox," pens, and a notepad. All else ought to be in the drawers, nicely organized.

Closets—If you haven't worn a clothing item in the last 12 months, say goodbye to it! (Here's where donating items can really be helpful to both you and someone in need.)

Affirm to yourself as you clear your clutter, "everything will be okay; it's safe to let go." It sounds silly, but clearing clutter is about letting go and trusting the process of life. Clutter holds us accountable for unresolved emotions like hurt, resentment, and other masks of fear.

In 2007, a new client, Alexandra, called for a feng shui consultation. She had three children who were acting out, and an estranged husband who she had just found out was cheating on her with an employee from their family-owned business, plus drug use and abuse from her husband were also involved. She was just beginning to file for divorce.

Immediately following her consultation, she started implementing my suggestions, one by one. Slowly, she started to see things change for the better in each area of her life. She was amazed to find that feng shui and spirit guidance interlocked to form a force field of protection, positive light, and emotion around and within her. Regarding one suggestion I'd given her, to clear out her bedroom closet, which was located in the Wealth section of her home, I asked her, "How can you walk into wealth if your closet is cluttered so badly that you literally can't even walk in a walk-in closet?" A few weeks later, she finally cleared it out and organized it. The day after cleaning it, she "walked into" $14,000, which is exactly what was needed for her lawyer's retainer and fees.

Clutter in the Body and the Mind

As a practicing nurse, I believe that when someone has a lot of clutter in their home, they oftentimes also have a lot of clutter ("waste") in their colon. And with that comes the underlying fear of letting go of the past, fear of letting go of control, and/or fear of letting go of that which no longer serves you. Regular colon-cleansing/clearing and eating the proper foods for your body are both essential for living a high quality of life. Look around at people with little clutter, and you will see they live a more active, healthier lifestyle . . . and have clear, radiant skin.

Mental clutter, too, will affect your life. Right now, to whatever extent you're doing it, stop criticizing, comparing, and judging yourself and others. Comparison breeds conflict. No good comes from sustaining an atmosphere in your mind that's cluttered with criticism and judgment. And to address another form of "mind clutter," stop worrying. Worry is a form of fear and will only prevent or slow down the solution that is coming.

Gossiping and complaining are other acts of mind clutter. They do no one any good. Besides, what you see in others is actually a mirror for the qualities of yourself. Make it a point to speak of others as if they were sitting right in front of you. You'll feel better doing this and it will keep you out of trouble. Speaking the truth in your words and speaking your mind—being loyal to your convictions and learning how to not take anything personally— have major positive-energy influences on your mind. My mottos are "Kill them with kindness," "Sprinkle them in fairy dust," and "Wish them blessings." These are all "kindness practices" that reap marvelous rewards for you and send out good energy to those around you.

The Gift of Spirit

~ 12 ~

The Gift of Grace

Grace is one of my favorite words in the English language. This chapter is about what grace is to me, and about how to make the most of the Gift of Grace. I believe grace is of the heart; it is pure love. To be in love is to be in grace. To feel and experience grace is to feel the opening of one's heart. It is a pure breath that expands the lungs fully, and then releases in an amazing calm . . . with a feeling of relief, stillness, and peace.

Grace, according to the *World English Dictionary*, is 1) beauty of form; 2) goodwill, favor; 3) prayer of thanks; 4) God's unmerited love for man. In my eyes, grace is God's love. And moving into a consciousness of Grace, we are freed from negativity, disillusionment, the ego's bondage, and false judgment.

Grace is the entwinement of forgiveness, enchantment, and gratitude, like a DNA chain. The spiral symbolizes that grace is eternal, and yet it moves in cycles; cycles of human condition, spiritual development, both on the individual and collective levels; and cycles of the cultivation of wisdom and true understanding.

While pregnant with my last child, I always seemed to be experiencing a unique state of grace. I even chose to name the baby Sophia Grace. (However, the baby turned out to be a boy, so I named him Steven Joseph, after my brother.) Even today, I have to say that when I'm in his presence, I experience an "amazing grace."

Forgiveness and Justice

Forgiveness—true forgiveness—engenders Grace. Whether the other person is sorry or not sorry, knows what they've done or not, is remorseful or vengeful, does not impact the need to forgive. It is important to recognize the importance of letting go, surrendering, and learning that holding onto the anguish, the hurt, the anger, and the fear that come from unforgiveness affects *you*. Unforgiveness deforms your personality and devastates your spirit, not theirs. The lesson of forgiveness further teaches us to just *stop* reacting to what happened in the past. Don't let a negative situation and/or negative people rob you of your well-being, your spirit, a vital part of your wholeness. By holding onto your role as "victim," you are ultimately letting "the perpetrator" win.

I believe forgiveness is a spiritual ideal. It becomes not a question of focusing or waiting for justice for the specific wrong committed; but rather a question of focusing on the form of your heart, the form of your healing, and your desires. The ideal is focused on what I call *faithful intellect*—living in the present and walking toward your future, *knowing* that you are doing the right thing and focusing on grace.

When you let go of judgment against people—yes, even though someone or something has wronged you in some way—you will release the negativity that glues you to the person or thing and become free from your bonds. Rip the daggers out from your own heart and lift them up to God. Wipe the blood off, wrap a bow around them, and send them back to where they came from, with acceptance and love, thus engendering peace . . . a true peace that brings forth grace.

Forgiveness and justice are separate entities. In some tarot decks, there is a Justice card, also known as the "Karma card." In the tarot, justice implies the ability to see all sides of the situation, a sort of overview, in order to bring forward positive thoughts and become able to make choices from a new perspective. Justice also implies accepting responsibility and turning inward to find a resolution—a new perspective, attitude, or behavior that will free you from the same old worn-out patterns of being, thinking, and acting that have affected your success in the recent past. As I mentioned in Chapter 4, "The Gift of Manifestation," owning up to your thoughts and actions sets in motion a universal energy force that supports a more just and righteous existence.

Seeking vengeance for a perceived wrong against you is not justice; it is an all-encompassing "hope trip" full of dark, dooming energy that is wasting your precious time and heart space. You are sitting there waiting for someone to acknowledge the wrong, whatever it may be. Let me be the first to tell you: don't hold your breath; it's not likely to happen.

My mother had an alcohol and prescription-pill problem after the deaths in my family. In the morning it was easy for me to forgive my mother for her doings of the previous day—but I didn't forget. I didn't think it was fair. But I always loved her. I always saw the struggle of her catastrophic life. There were, however, many years of anger and lack of forgiveness toward my mother, related to my childhood and even early adulthood.

When I was in my early to mid twenties, I thought and would often proclaim aloud about my own mother, "She doesn't even see the wrong; she doesn't remember the abuse to even have a chance to acknowledge it, to offer me true repentance. Where's the justice in that?!" I would tell her about how she'd abused me, because she wouldn't remember half the time and she would apologize the next day. But in time, apologies tend to grow transparent and meaningless when the abusive behavior continues day after day.

It wasn't until I reached twenty-eight years of age that I just "got it" one day. I was looking in the wrong place the whole time for the justice I was seeking. I learned to let go of my anger and my unforgiveness, and I had an epiphany: that it was really all right, that I could change my perspective on this injustice to a state of acceptance and grace. This was clearly the moment of forgiveness, where the pain stopped, where the hurt melted away and left a painless scar. Mind you, I have a scar that's visible to the eye to remind me of the pain that once was; but it also reminds me of the grace and forgiveness that bestowed itself upon me.

Recall moments of grace you've experienced by way of forgiving someone or something, and reflect upon each instance's value to your life. Remember the past, but *don't live in it*. The point of remembering, in my case, is so that I can look back and rewrite or reframe my wound. I know that my mother didn't mean her actions or words. They were coming from an unfathomable depth of pain that she had masked with alcohol and pills.

Nothing happens that isn't supposed to happen—all of our experiences are part of our destiny. Every experience, both light and dark, "good" and "bad," comes to be experienced fully for the betterment of your soul and moves you closer to the center of your target of "happily ever after." Don't dwell on past wrongs one moment longer without finding forgiveness, because with forgiveness, you are letting go of that which cannot possibly serve your highest good. You're letting go of the emotions that once held strong negative power over you.

The moment you truly forgive, you feel like a burden has been lifted off of not only your shoulders, but also your heart. You know the pain is gone. The space that once was full of hollowness and hurt is now filled with grace. You feel an "okay-ness" with the knowledge that compassion will soon follow.

Compassion

Having compassion goes along with grace and forgiveness like a horse and carriage. Through the grace of God, I eventually was instilled with compassion for my mother, age-appropriate understanding, and a heart that remained open to heal and to love. You must have compassion and love for yourself in order to be able to apply compassion and love to another. Any situation can be healed by letting go of judgment. Instead of seeing someone as "good" or "bad," have compassion for all, and know that everyone is doing the best they can. Instead of pitying someone, see that person's inner strength and Godliness. In that way, you encourage divine light to be expressed within the other person and yourself. Every day is a chance to clear away ego, forget judgment, and act lovingly and responsibly with compassion.

Enchantment

True enchantment comes from pure love . . . a kind of love that flows from your core, channeled through you from the Universe itself. Enchantment is about living in truth and goodness with the knowledge that our cups overflow with love. This love can only be described as *enchanting*.

Being enchanted comes from spiritual love. How do we become filled with this? One must look beyond the confines of their religion and anything that limits them to a church or any one book or set of books. Beyond that point you can discover true enchantment.

I think that, subconsciously, we're all longing for a life filled with more meaning and the sheer beauty of enchantment. Every tree, stone, person, animal, mountain, ocean, and stream—all of these things that we have been blessed with—carry the Gift of Grace through enchantment. There is a pure love connecting all of these things to the wholeness of God's magnificent creation. Look at everything with awe, wonder, and delight, and you will submerge yourself and your perception into the stream of enchantment.

I often envision myself as a little girl, a child of God. I am continually learning and open to being in a state of goodness, working to stay balanced and centered, whirling a glittering magic wand and knowing that *love is the law*. To live in gratitude and in a state of grace, we must accept that *love is the law* and offer ourselves to be of service to this principle.

Each of us is the same, at the level of unity, oneness, and wholeness. However, we are also different. The joy of discovery and the vehicle by which one becomes "enchanted" are different for each person. My enchantment has been my unfolding truth and, along the way, I have chosen to discover more, to surrender more, and to let the universe unfold before and within my heart. Unbeknownst to my "ego-self," I came upon a realm of grace I never knew existed. Each of us is born unto this world with a different core. And that core, your soul, has a specific question you were born to answer, to discover: a *quest*-ion, if you will. It is in the act of surrendering and witnessing the grandeur of the realm of grace that you may come to pop "the big question" of your life. For me, the "big question" is and has always been, *What is the meaning and purpose of this life?* Which of the following big questions resonates with your core? Meditate, contemplate, and perhaps journal on the following questions:

- What is my purpose in this life?

- How can I perfect myself? How am I different from other beings?

- What is the meaning of life and death?

- How can I battle and transcend the ego and live in universal love and truth?

- Where am I going? What do I have to do to survive?

Recognizing Opportunities for Grace

The evening of September 10, 2001, was a calm one at home, with the sounds of my children delightfully playing, laundry quietly spinning, and dishes clanking in preparation for dinner. The phone rang, and my then-husband, Tom, answered it, and soon looked to me and said, "It's your ex-husband . . . again."

"Again?! I've already spoken to him a few times today." I accepted his phone call.

He said, "I'm getting ready to board the plane for New York in a few moments and I have to tell you, I really need you to hear me. I have to say, I'm sorry for abandoning you and I apologize for hurting you so deeply. I need for you to know that I will always love you."

I was a bit nervous at this point. Some of the anxiety was because he called a number of times that day to tell me some pretty deep sentiments in front of Tom at the time (and I wasn't sure what Tom's reaction to all this might be). Apart from that, I felt anxiety that maybe something was wrong with the plane or something bad might happen in New York.

Jim and I had been divorced for a few years. After the divorce he had moved to Orlando from Tampa, having accepted a new job with Morgan Stanley Dean Witter & Co. He was going to a one-day training workshop at the company headquarters at the Twin Towers in New York. I closed the telephone conversation light-heartedly, "You're making me a little nervous, now. Listen: everything is going to be fine! Good luck with your new training, and thank you for your apology."

The next morning, September 11, I was at work, sitting in my L-shaped cubicle. I heard an "Oh, my God" in a fearful, shocked voice from a person in the cubicle behind me. Tom worked in the same office. He walked over to my desk and said in a quiet panic, "Tina, a plane just flew into the Twin Towers."

I sat there in my chair without moving, trying to digest what had just happened. I believe all I said was, "Okay, okay; it's okay."

A few moments later, Tom came again and said, "Tina, I'm so sorry; the other tower was just hit, too."

I maintained a calm facade, but said, "He's in there. I know it." I was thinking, though, *For sure, he's dead, especially taking into account his behavior on the phone yesterday.* I went over the phone conversations I'd had with Jim, like rewinding a movie and pushing the play button again and again.

He was in Twin Tower II, in the cafeteria on the 44th floor, taking a break, when they were told to evacuate. *What's going on?* he wondered, as he heard shouts of, "A helicopter flew into the other tower" and "No, it's a bomb!"

Sensing the panic and hysteria rumble through the crowd as people made their way to the stairwell, he decided to take the elevator back up to the 61st floor where his training workshop was being held, to get his phone and wallet. As he made it to that floor, he was quickly rerouted back to the stairwells. A voice over the loudspeaker explained that their building was not affected, but was to be evacuated. This gave little or no relief; people remained scared and frantically hustling down the endless flights of stairs. Just a few moments later, the building of Tower II shook with an explosion. The emergency lights flashing throughout the packed staircase were accompanied by the smell of raw, crumbling construction. Jim stood still and the wall of the building slammed right into him. He said it felt like an earthquake. Structural damage was visible immediately—cracks and bulges in the cement.

Everyone around him was in complete panic mode. His reaction was to stay calm and collected, even though he, too, was fearful that this was the end—that he was going to die that day. Having spent a couple of years training for the military at West Point, he went into a distinctive "soldier" mode. He wrapped his arms around a sobbing woman who was having a difficult time walking. She was calling out her fiancée's name, knowing that he was on one of the higher floors. They kept moving down the flights of stairs, passing an older, heavy-set woman sitting in a state of exhaustion on the ground—she would never make it out as she was. But the sobbing woman wouldn't let go of him; she remained clinging to him for her life. He made the split-second decision to continue going down the stairs with the woman who wouldn't let go. Suddenly, another woman came out of nowhere, shouting and crying. Jim held the two women as he quickened his steps out of the building to safety. At this point policeman and fireman were pouring inside.

He kept thinking of the heavyset woman who couldn't climb down any farther; so he thought he would go back in. When he turned and starting back into the building, one of the ladies whom he just escorted out clung to his arm with all the strength she could muster. She begged him, "No, no, you can't go back in; you'll die!"

He decided not to go back in. Within a few more moments, that tower completely collapsed. A few hours later, Jim had made it through the rubble to a pay phone and dialed my company's toll-free number, letting me know that he had made it out alive.

And while the tragic and devastating events of that Tuesday morning left him with traumatic visions that would recur in his consciousness, he was not angry or bitter or filled with a desire for retaliation. He believed, like I did, that a war would only bring more pain. He had an opportunity for grace and he took it. He said he felt grace—grace about every living thing. He even went for a walk through Central Park the next day, smiling just because he was alive. He experienced the Gift of Grace.

I'm positive that each one of us can recall where we were and exactly what we were doing when we heard about the attacks. It was a remarkable tragedy and a time of darkness in our nation, and in the world as a whole. After September 11, the war on Iraq began, kicking off a full-blown, long-lasting battle that has expanded into Afghanistan and has killed thousands. Our country embarked on a retaliatory, vengeful, and violent journey. What justice could truly be served by going to war? This cannot be how a country gets justice. True justice comes from grace, not from warfare.

What would our world be like if we had used grace and forgiveness instead of responding with a full-out war? What would have been the result if, instead of using the same vile energy, the same terror and horror as the enemy who came against us, we sought to respond with grace and forgiveness? We have all seen, some of us firsthand, the death, the fear, and the agony this war has brought to our nation and the people of Iraq and Afghanistan. By going to war looking for revenge, we are only killing more of our precious citizens and wounding the hearts of more of our families. I'm certainly not saying we should not go after the people who participated in this terrorism. I'm saying we should use this darkness, this grief that has consumed us, and heal together, getting closer together in grace as a country and as a worldwide family. We could have used our resources to spread grace like wildfire instead of spreading death, degradation, and starvation.

To read this is one thing, but to live it is another. Practice living in grace, with forgiveness, compassion, enchantment, generosity, and love. These aren't just words; these are the gifts that make our beautiful earth go around.

May the Gift of Grace be ours from this day forward, forever and ever. . . .

～ 13 ～

The Gift of Healing

We each have the power within us to heal in an all-encompassing way—physically, emotionally, and spiritually. The first step is to recognize your emotions: connect with how you're truly feeling inside, and feel those emotions fully. Then it's a matter of knocking out any guilt and other negative setback emotions with one good punch!

The single most important connection I have made regarding healing and physical disease is that the root of all physical disease is specifically related to your thoughts and emotions. All disease ultimately stems from fear released through negative emotions—such as anger, guilt, shame, and resentment—and negative thoughts and beliefs. To experience disease is to experience a total or partial disconnection from wholeness, from Oneness, through our attachment to the negative energies associated with fear and separation from Spirit. You see, the Universe supports both our thoughts and our emotions, so it is imperative to look within ourselves to understand that we hold the key to our own wellness and healing or our own sickness and ill health. We need to search within to see what is going on in our lives that might be causing any disease or illness we might be experiencing. Physical disease is our body's way of calling our awareness to the emotions and beliefs that no longer serve our health.

Louise Hay, in her best-selling book *You Can Heal Your Life*, put it in a nutshell:

> The universe supports us in every thought we choose to think and believe. As children, we learn from our parents and those around us how to think and feel about ourselves and life. When we grow up, we tend to re-create what is familiar to us, and so we end up reinforcing and drawing to us that which supports our original views and feelings about ourselves and life. Physical diseases, then, are the body's way of calling attention to thoughts, beliefs and feelings we're holding (consciously or unconsciously) that are no longer serving—and are actually "toxic" to—our present state of being.

Our bodies are trying to say something to us. The disease itself is the red flag saying, "Hello; pay attention to me! I'm trying to tell you something!"

Another excellent aspect of *You Can Heal Your Life* is that it offers the reader a "dictionary of ailments" *and* a guide to identify the mental patterns or emotional issues that create disease in the body. It's a great book to open the doors for recognizing and understanding the disease process as it relates to your thoughts/beliefs, emotions, and spirituality.

The example of Christopher and Dana Reeve has certainly touched my heart. Christopher Reeve (the actor who depicted Superman in the 1978 version of *Superman*) died in October 2004. Not even a year later, after losing her husband, Dana was diagnosed with lung cancer (and would die of it in March 2006). Even though she was a nonsmoker, it made perfect sense to me. She loved him so dearly, she couldn't *breathe* without him. It was only fitting that her deep-seated feelings of grief would affect her lungs. It's an amazingly sad but true love story. Dana, who released this statement in August 2005, felt the Gift of Spirit through her late husband, Christopher:

> Now, more than ever, I feel Chris with me as I face this challenge. As always, I look to him as the ultimate example of defying the odds with strength, courage and hope in the face of life's adversities. (*www.usatoday.com/life/people/2005-08-09-reeve-cancer_x.htm*)

Many times, when a person loses a husband or wife, sibling or child, the one left living suffers a broken heart from the loved one's passing, thus developing heart problems and often dying of a heart attack—literally dying of a broken heart.

After the passing of my brother Steven, I developed two stomach ulcers and constipation. At the young age of seven, I watched, rapt, as my mother become a basket case over my brother's death; I couldn't comprehend why and where my brother actually went. My ailments make sense: I couldn't "digest" the situation. The problems with my stomach stemmed from my unassuaged fear, and the severe constipation came from an inability to understand the "circle of life" and to assimilate change.

At age thirteen, a few months after the passing of both my father and my brother Kevin, I broke out with huge patches of psoriasis on my stomach and back. They were perfectly round patches, like someone had shot me through my stomach and out my back. In the years of stress that followed, the psoriasis proceeded to cover my head. Looking back at what happened; I now see that my skin condition was my body's way of saying, "I'm scared now, and I fear I'm going to be hurt."

Look at your own life and try to correlate the emotional and physical events. Fear is a particularly prominent emotion involved in the generation of disease. We can use a wide variety of healing modalities to address our fears—or any debilitating emotions or beliefs/thought patterns—before they manifest as physical disease. In the following sections I will briefly explain several modalities that I have learned and used in my practice. I would, however, like to recommend that you research further those modalities you are drawn to. Today you might be specifically drawn to one that can help with something you're currently concerned about; and then perhaps next month, or next year, you will be drawn to different modalities. This process is ultimately where you start to use your own intuition to facilitate healing.

Acupuncture and Chinese Medicine

Acupuncture and traditional Chinese medicine (TCM) don't approach the signs and symptoms of a disease the way "Western" medicine does. They look directly to the "inner" source, the source from which the disease came, and they do so without the use of drugs or invasive procedures.

Diary Entry: July 6, 2006

I made an appointment for acupuncture following my recent diagnosis of severe anemia. This would be my first personal experience with acupuncture. The lady acupuncturist's name was Sharon. She had a plain physical appearance and a very kind presence and an aura that spoke of peace and knowledge. The exam room was bright, with an entire wall made of window that was covered with gray, metal mini-blinds partially opened and overlooking the parking lot. She did her assessment and explained that my skin condition, psoriasis, is linked to the lung, and the emotion of grief. And the anemia stemmed from this same emotion, as well. She then explained she was going to start out with four needles today.

I lay face up on my back on the exam table, while she placed these four needles at specific points on my body. She put soft healing music on, placed an infrared light that hovered an inch above my legs, and said she was going to leave me alone for 10 minutes. As she left the room, I started thinking in amazement about my meditation from that morning, which had focused around the grief card (from my personal tarot meditation cards) as my psychological environment. I had explained to her the history of my psoriasis and my childhood, as well as my present

---

ailments around anemia, which I felt was reflecting my current relationships.

Within a few moments, I was suddenly overwhelmed with the emotion of pure grief. It all made sense. A recent relationship had reminded me of my childhood, and I found myself for the past few months in sadness, crying for my father as I did when I was a young girl after he had died. I lay there flat on my back with that infrared light over my lower legs so I didn't dare move an inch. I lay perfectly still, letting the tears build up and roll off my eyes, as I felt my grief come up to be healed. Then something amazing happened. My father's spirit came right through the window, through the blinds. I felt him touch my head with his big strong hand.

"It's okay," he said as I felt him caress my forehead with long, firm strokes, "Remember to hang in there. It's okay, it's okay, it's okay."

As he spoke, tears kept falling from my eyes, like a stream. I calmed myself down and took a couple of deep breaths. Sharon walked back in the room a few moments later, and worked on my neck, then removed the needles. She said I did excellent for the first visit. Indeed, I did. A very healing experience had taken place that day, for which I was ever so grateful.

In the same way that Louise Hay suggests one seek out the specific emotional "obstacle" to the flow of health and vitality, acupuncture and TCM seek to discover and "resolve" energy blockages to the flow of chi within a person. The natural, unimpeded flow of chi is the goal of the acupuncturist or practitioner of TCM; in this way, a balance of energy is restored within the individual, resulting in a life of wellness and wholeness.

The concepts of "Western" medicine have begun to shift in recent years. Acupuncture and TCM have become treasures that are marveled at throughout the world. Many TCM practitioners have established an excellent reputation in the West for their effective treatment of illnesses and disorders.

Aromatherapy

Aromatherapy also has the objective of enlivening the whole person; in this healing modality, it is done by "letting one's nose lead the way." Your sense of smell is a passageway to the "underground" of your intuition. People who are highly intuitive typically have an amazing sense of smell. As you embark on freeing yourself from the clutter of your mind, physical body, and spirit, you will most likely notice that your sense of smell and the taste on your palate are heightened and have more of a "clean" feeling. Having done feng shui consultations and studied alternative methods of healing for many years, I have continually used scent as a means to not only improve overall health, but also to target specific ailments and to elevate the spirit.

The best ways I've found to incorporate aromatherapy are to use essential oils: put them in an oil burner/diffuser, add them to bath water, mix them into massage oil and apply it through massage, or to add a drop on a washcloth or pillow case. There are also flower waters, incense, and herbs that can be explored, per your personal preferences and inclinations.

Aromatherapy works magic on the body, mind, and spirit. It broadens your healing horizons. The following are my most used aromatherapy oils and what they are used for:

> *Bergamot*—Elevates the spirit and clarifies the mind. Assists with confidence and inner strength. It's relaxing and can even help reduce fever. Often used in men's fragrances.

> *Eucalyptus*—Banishes negative energy. Used for physical healing and purification. Great for upper-respiratory infections, sinus problems, and congestion.

> *Frankincense*—Considered an offering to God and the angelic realm; used for purification and the awakening of spiritual understanding. Helps overcome feelings of fear, loss, and grief.

> *Grapefruit*—Assists in self-confidence and clarity, as well as in overcoming the pain of past experiences dealing with jealousy and bitterness. This is a great one to use to heal and let go of a past relationship.

> *Lavender*—Used for inner peace and uplifting the spirit, and for health, mental clarity, and new beginnings. This is probably the most widely used essential oil.

> *Vanilla*—Opens the heart chakra to love and stimulates energy and mental powers.

Ylang-ylang—Attracts love and enhances sensuality. Assists in development of self-worth and self-confidence. Helps let go of negative emotions, such as anger, guilt, and resentment.

Animal Spirit Energies

Using and becoming aware of animal spirit energy is another way to open your heart, mind, and soul to receiving the messages of Spirit. I have found that when someone has an experience with an animal or has repeated sightings of the same animal, whether in a physical or symbolic form, the animal spirit energies are trying to convey a message or offer healing or guidance from Spirit. (For in-depth discussions of animal spirits, I recommend *Animal Spirit Guides* by Steven D. Farmer and *Animal-Speak* by Ted Andrews.)

Many animals that have come across my path in physical form have guided me, helped me heal, protected me and/or encouraged me. I remember driving from St. Augustine to Tampa and seeing three deer standing in perfect alignment alongside the interstate. I knew then the power of the three, being my brothers' and father's spirit, but also knew the power and meaning of the deer: When deer show up in your life, they can signal an opportunity for gentle love, or a gentle invitation to new adventure. Deer also can bring the message of trusting your intuition. They often offer a simple, gentle reassurance. When I saw the three deer that day, I felt just that: a gentle reassurance from their spirit. I felt that the message from Spirit was to reaffirm my trust and my intuition regarding the forward movement in my life (which turned out to provide the impetus for a very important healing phase for me).

I've had the great fortune of many personal experiences like these . . . experiences that have led me to a deep and abiding appreciation for the magic and mystery of animals. From furry rabbits running through the fields to the beautiful flying vultures soaring in the clear blue sky, and everything in between, my consciousness is truly connected to the healing, revealing power of all animals.

Animals can also come to you in symbolic form in inner visions, meditations, and dreams. One day in April 2007, I was doing a weekend psychic fair at a local New Age store. I and another lady were both doing intuitive angel readings. There was also an astrologer and an intuitive reader named Cathy, who set up an artist station to do animal and chakra drawings. Cathy was able to feel, see, and hear messages from people's particular animal spirit guides. She also had the ability to read energy by holding jewelry (a form of psychometry).

In between readings when things were slow, we had time to talk to one another and exchange readings. After giving Cathy an angel reading, I sat down at her table and she began drawing a lemur.

"Yes, you're definitely the lemur," she said in a confident tone, showing me the animal she drew. She explained that the lemur represents powers of clairvoyance, that mine were becoming increasingly powerful, and that—through the presence of the lemurian energy—I am able to see spirits clearly (which was correct). She went on to say that what others first notice about me is my penetrating green eyes (which are notable traits of lemurs). She added that my uniqueness sometimes makes me feel out of place with others, and that I need to seek out the comfort of solitude. I found all of these observations to be remarkably true. But she wasn't done yet; the rest of her reading carries us straight into a discussion of gemstones.

Gemstones

Cathy, the intuitive artist, went on to hold rings I was wearing on each ring finger. I had just purchased a brand new David Yurman ring; the center stone was a prasiolite surrounded by little diamonds and set in silver. I had been eyeing this ring for a few months at Saks Fifth Avenue, and was so pleased with the purchase. I felt a strong connection to this piece, and did research as to what the gemstone prasiolite meant. I found that the prasiolite offers a connection between heavenly and earthly realms. It facilitates the gap between the physical and spiritual aspects of life. It also attracts prosperity, and turned out to be perfect for me in every way. I found this ring just one month after the passing of my mother. I felt strongly that she wanted me to have it, as though it would offer a connection to my family now that they all were in Spirit while I remained, for now, here on earth.

Cathy also felt the prasiolite energy was connected to my heart chakra and was radiating out something wonderful. (I'll discuss chakras in detail in the next section.) Then she focused on my other ring: an emerald set in yellow gold. It is an antique in an estate-piece setting and has a uniquely tiered rectangle shape in the highest center level, then a lower-tier level of diamonds to the side of the center emerald. The ring was once my mother's, and has a special meaning and feeling for me. Cathy said the ring connected to my fourth chakra and to my core, catching and manifesting light from there.

Whether it is a standalone piece of stone or a stone set as jewelry, a gemstone's value is the same. Take a look at what stones you are drawn to and become aware of their meaning. What stones or special pieces of jewelry do you have and love to wear? What meaning do they convey to you? You will then be able to learn and create conscious awareness of healing through these gemstones.

Gemstones can be used as a way of healing (also called crystal healing); energy can transfer from the gemstone into the body. Gemstones can aid in the release of physical conditions and emotional unbalances. They can also be used in dissolving blockages to emotional expression. For example, in both modern gemstone healing and TCM (which dates back over 5,000 years), magnetite has an energetic affinity to ears, bones, and kidneys; iron pyrite is useful with bone-related problems and fractures; and hematite can be used as a healing agent for blood conditions and sleeping problems.

Gemstones can be used in a variety of ways: you can wear them as jewelry on the body, carry around a gemstone that feels particularly resonant, place a gemstone in your bath or on your nightstand, or keep it close to your body or slip it under your pillow. With the right intentions and awareness, gemstones can rebalance and realign one's physical, emotional, or spiritual energy to correct disease.

Here are my top gemstones and their meanings.

Amethyst—Amethyst is a vibrant purple stone, the color of the "third eye" chakra, making it a perfect stone for meditation and inspiration. Since it is known for being the "stone of spirituality and happiness," it brings strength and the purest form of peace.

The color purple in feng shui is the color for wealth and royalty, so that is another additional benefit to this stone. With its meditative qualities and balancing of the psyche, it can help with alcoholism or any other addictive behavior. It also helps treat disorders of the heart, stomach, skin, teeth, and nervous system.

Blue topaz—Blue topaz carries the energy of being able to see "the big picture, the grand scheme." It is also known as the stone for love and success, transforming fear and negativity into love and optimism. Blue topaz aids the throat chakra, bringing clarity to one's verbalization and communication, and it has the trickle-down effects of promoting individuality and creativity. Additionally, it holds energy that can facilitate the laws of attraction and manifestation. It helps with any kind of skin eruption or disorder, balances the senses, and brings the body, mind, and spirit into union.

Celestite—This is my favorite free-standing stone. (It generally comes in chunks too large to be used in jewelry or the like.) Celestite symbolizes spiritual development, enlightenment, empathy, prayer, openness, clarity of thought, and purity of heart. It provides a connection to our heavenly guardian angels and the angelic realms. It's no wonder, since the colors typically found in this stone are hues of heavenly sparkly blues and baby blues. When you give this stone as a gift in the spirit of love, it brings love, light, peace, and harmony. It is also said to be "fairy dust of good fortune" and can facilitate physical healing related to digestive, intestinal, and stomach disorders.

Diamond—The diamond, known as the hardest natural stone on earth, is the ultimate gem. It is known to be given as a pledge of loyalty and love, a symbol of forming an unbreakable bond. Diamonds can be used to remind us of spiritual awareness and the fruition of manifestation of the passions of one's heart. The positive spiritual energy from wearing a diamond can be passed on to others. In healing terms, diamonds can help strengthen one's body and spirit, and can be used for clarity of mind and the development of both physical and spiritual sight.

Emerald—Emerald attracts prosperity. It also has a harmonious and calming effect and balances the heart chakra. The emerald-green hue of the "green room" where actors go to wait and rest is said to be soothing and helps with nerves and diminishing anxiety, much as this stone does. Emeralds also increase one's intuitive ability and are used to heal heart conditions, both emotional and physical, as well as problems associated with the lungs.

Prasiolite—Prasiolite helps to link the physical and spiritual aspects of life. It activates the heart as the center of consciousness and strengthens the mind, emotions, and will. Prasiolite also aids one in illumination, germination, and completion; seeing a task, dream, or mission through to the end. In healing, prasiolite offers self-courage and emotional support.

Rose quartz—Rose quartz emits a gentle loving energy, representing unconditional love; it heals and opens one's heart, facilitating a deep inner healing, especially in correlation with positive affirmation work. It holds qualities of self-love, self-forgiveness, self-confidence, and fertility. Physically, it can help with vertigo and disorders of the kidneys, hormones, or adrenal glands.

Chakras

Getting to know your chakras is an amazing way to develop a connection between the physical and spiritual aspects of yourself. Chakras are vital energy centers shaped like circles that surround the physical body. These energy centers are also known as the aura, or etheric body. Pretend you are wearing a crown; these energy centers run from the top of the crown down to the base of your spine and sacrum, and through your lower extremities.

There are seven major chakras, each of which correlates with specific organ systems in the body and different emotional states. It is important to understand the triad connection of one's spirit, emotions, and physical body.

Each of the seven chakras is associated with and assigned to specific parts of your physical body. Different emotional stresses and physical diseases can be reflected in and affect one of your seven chakras. These effects can be diagnosed specifically and can then be evaluated and assessed for recognition and healing. (*Women's Bodies, Women's Wisdom* by Christiane Northrup, M.D. has a wonderful and informative section on chakras.) A basic understanding of your chakras and how they function is essential to the healing of both body and spirit.

The First Chakra—Location: Base of spine, sacrum. Chakra energy: Grounding to physical life, connection to earth, foundation, and family. Associated color: Red. Treatment stones: Red jasper, onyx, bloodstone.

The Second Chakra—Location: Pelvis and reproductive organs. Chakra energy: Creativity, money, base of passions, reproduction. Associated color: Orange. Treatment stones: Orange carnelian or calcite, topaz.

The Third Chakra—Location: Stomach, liver, adrenals, pancreas. Chakra energy: Self-esteem, personal power, sifting through and analyzing emotions. Associated color: Yellow. Treatment stones: Citrine, amber, tiger's eye.

The Fourth Chakra—Location: Heart, lungs, ribs, shoulders. Chakra energy: Opens the heart to love. Associated colors: Green, pink. Treatment stones: Rose and green quartz, jade.

The Fifth Chakra—Location: Thyroid, throat, neck, mouth. Chakra energy: Communication, self-expression, will. Associated color: Blue. Treatment stones: Turquoise, blue topaz, blue lace agate.

The Sixth Chakra—Location: Eyes, between and above the eyebrows ("third eye"), ears, nose. Chakra energy: Clarity, vision of the third eye, intuition, wisdom. Associated color: Indigo. Treatment stones: Lapis lazuli, sodalite, moldavite.

The Seventh Chakra—Location: The crown (top of head). Chakra energy: Peace, intuitive connection, awakened consciousness, connection to the divine. Associated color: Violet. Treatment stones: Amethyst, celestite, clear quartz.

Visualization

I mentioned visualization as a process of manifestation. Visualization can additionally be a part of the healing process. Practice visualization in accordance with the specifics of your emotional and physical aspects that require healing.

When my children turn up with a fever, I tuck them into bed and practice visualization as one step of the healing process (along with a "healing massage" technique and an affirmation, as discussed in Chapter 6, "The Gift of Children"). I have them think about being in the purest of snow, lying down, making snow angels with their bodies, and playing in the snow. I also ask them to visualize the prettiest snowflakes falling from the sky all around them. They typically wake up the next morning with their fever gone.

Try something as simple as showering—visualize optimal health radiating through your body and showering your body with health: a rain of positivity, or a rain of cleansing "fairy dust," washing away all illness and negativity. Visualize the sickness, disease, and any negative emotion coming off of you, and all of it going right down into the drain.

The same thing can be done with bathing, especially in Epsom salts (which draw out toxins and reduce inflammation) or any aromatherapy bath. Be conscious of what you're bathing in and why. Visualize the water as being a conduit of ultimate cleansing.

Going Green

When we do our part in healing ourselves, we can then become more aware of the earth and therefore more able to contribute to the healing of the earth as a whole. That, in turn, becomes a further part of our own healing. Going green—using environmentally friendly products, recycling, and conserving energy and water—are all magnificent ways to affect the earth we live on. To know that doing our seemingly tiny part is contributing to saving this big, beautiful world is an amazing and uplifting feeling. So green up your lifestyle and make a difference!

All of these modalities offer healing of the physical, emotional, and spiritual kind. Explore these different avenues for developing wellness, and you will discover a great road to healing and wholeness. There is a plethora of knowledge out there for you to research, and many avenues for you to explore.

⟨ 14 ⟩

The Gift of Affirmations

An affirmation is simply a positive statement or asser-
tion "affirming" a desirable objective, goal, or ideal.
Similarly, an affirmation prayer is a positive statement
and request that is released in prayer form to God/Spirit.

What can affirmations do? What are they good for?
In my experience, affirmations can seep into your mind
and become little droplets of peace, positive direction,
hope, reassurance, and healing, as well as seeds of manifestation. Affirmations can change your mindset, and
soon you'll find that these little droplets have enlivened
in you an ocean of positive thinking, positive acting, and
positive being. This ocean contains the ebb and flow of
both more enlightened being and more complete healing. How grand is that?! All from starting with a few positive statements.

Affirmations are one of the concepts my clients and
the people around me seem to put up the most resistance
to grasping. Yet using affirmations is so simple! Let's
practice a basic affirmation exercise to beckon some self-
realization. For instance, say aloud the following
affirmation:

"I am a channel for God, and my work reflects my higher good."

Then ask yourself, *Do I believe this is true?* Regardless of the confidence level of your response, just by saying this affirmation, you can start to open your mind to your connection to God/Spirit and really become conscious of the value and magnitude of your work. Soon your work will reflect this opening of your mind to a more conscious contact with the divine, and will bring forward positive changes in your attitude toward your work.

Another simple affirmation, related to the previous one, aims to align you with the best possible view of yourself in the work/occupation you do. Here is the one I use:

"I, Tina Coluccio, am a brilliant and prolific writer."

Add your own name and personalize it to express the work/job you do in the highest, most ideal terms, just the way I did.

The Gift of Affirmations in my life has shown up in many different areas. One particularly noteworthy example occurred in 2007 at a time when I desperately needed money. I was in the process of divorcing my second husband and found myself in a holding pattern for a few months, paying the mortgage and overhead by myself during a period of uncertain income. I had fallen short on my mortgage payment and other household expenses while trying to pay attorney fees. I made up an affirmation for prosperity that may sound silly, although my children love it . . . and it worked!

I said (and continue to say, whenever I use it), "I wish, I wish, with all my heart, there will be a check in the mail . . . in the mailbox so dark."

And even though it sounds like a wishing rhyme, I affirm there will be a check in the mail, meaning I will receive abundance. So, one day after picking up the children from school, I pulled into the driveway and started saying this affirmation out loud while walking to the mail box. I opened the mailbox and found an envelope with my mortgage company's name on it. I opened it, and lo and behold, it was an escrow overage check for 2,600 dollars. And the best part of it all was seeing a message from the Gift of Spirit come through—that is, the check's date was 01/04/07. Those are "my numbers" from Spirit (numbers I've associated Spirit messages with since the time of my awakening to my family members' spiritual presence). The following day, *another* check came from the closing of a bank investment—600 dollars—and the check number was 147! These checks *reaffirmed* to me that the power of affirmations and the power of my faith in God and Spirit created an exquisitely timed, divine landing of abundance, like a plane flying in with a gracious gift of prosperity on its wings, ending my holding pattern.

Millions of people use affirmations on a daily basis. In the preceding chapter, "The Gift of Healing," I mention Louise Hay, a renowned New Age author, who uses and teaches the importance of affirmations to change your thinking from negative to positive with the use of positive statements and affirmations. Her book *You Can Heal Your Life* alone has sold over 35 million copies! (And it's a must-have book in my home.) This is just a small bit of evidence of the power of affirmations, another sacred gift of Spirit.

The following is a sort of "workshop affirmation." To start out, play the role of a doctor—more specifically, a cardiologist. Examine your heart, and assess the amount of love in your life. Are you giving love as well as receiving love? In what ways might you be holding back love to another? In what ways are you holding back love from yourself? Do you love with strings attached? Sometimes my clients have had recent chest pain or are lashing out in small outbursts of anger. I am here to tell you what I tell them: love has real power. Love cannot be bottled and served on the rocks or served up as a pill to swallow. Love is the sacred energy of life itself, of Spirit moving within and between us. Love can be the most powerful medicine if you can surrender to the opening and examination of your own heart. Love is all there is when you let everything else go. Many of us neglect ourselves by not taking care of our own needs. Babies do not survive when they are neglected—in medical terms, it is called, "failure to thrive"; as adults, we are responsible for ensuring we thrive. We need to balance between nurturing and loving ourselves, as well as nurturing and loving others. To that end, what follows are some effective affirmations and affirmation prayers I have used myself and with my clients for years. May they bring to you the same positive effects they have brought to me.

Affirmations

"Love flows freely through me, and I am filled with divine light and love. I breathe love in and I breathe love out." (Say aloud and take deep breath in and out.) "And I am at peace."

"I honor my physical body. I honor myself. I am a beautiful being."

"I love and honor myself, making a gateway and clear path for others to love me. I am open and receptive to both giving and receiving energies of love."

"I am open and ready to receive all the prosperity in the Universe." (Hold your hands out as you say this affirmation.)

"I allow myself to uplift and move to a better place. I am worthy. I forgive myself and others. My heart is forgiving, light, and free."

"I am financially secure. I have mastery over the material aspects of my life. I am supported and will always be provided for—in the present and every day in the future."

"I am worthy of and deserve to receive goodness and abundance at all times."

"Everything is in divine and perfect order. I am at the perfect moment in time. Only right and good things are taking place in my life."

"My home is filled with peace and love."

"My work is filled with harmony and prosperity."

"I am conscious of my thoughts, and my thoughts will become form. I have incredible power and wonder that spirals inward, building hope, and creating freedom and healing."

"Each day is a new beginning, a new chance to expect a miracle. May we all feel truly heaven-blessed."

"I am open to receiving help, to receiving a miracle. With faith and God, all things are possible."

"I am free and I am truly powerful. I allow myself to enjoy this freedom and power with grace and love."

"God/Spirit is with me and engendering a miracle. I am safe and protected at all times."

"I am confident and successful. I move forward into a new and positive beginning—seeing from a new perspective—into a new and fresh phase of life and opportunities for growth."

"I release anything that is negative. I release anything that is not love. I choose today to find peace, hope, and joy in every day."

"I leave the entanglements of my mind. I shut out all discordance and fear, and rise into the consciousness of light. I turn my face up toward the golden sun, breathing in the warm light with a deep breath. I am perfect; I am love." (Hold your hands out as you say this affirmation.)

"I release all negative thoughts and judgments about myself and others, and focus on the love and grace that is within all."

"With faith, all things are possible. I deserve the best and I release my worries, anxiety and fears to God."

"Through these twisted turns of fate, I remain centered in the eye of the storm, centered in faith and gratitude, in order to find clarity and open the door to my desires."

Affirmation Prayers

"God/Blessed Spirit, please shield me and protect me against all enemies. I humbly ask that my prayers be heard and answered. I thank thee for all thy infinite goodness. Please grant me my humble petitions to the stars in the night sky."

"I ask for the courage and the strength to carry on. Please grant me clarity and wisdom. Help me trust that when all of the pieces fall into place, I will understand and see clearly. Please be with me—I ask this in your name. Amen."

"Perfect, Ever Holy Spirit/God, mercifully heed our cries and our sadness. Heal our sorrows, our afflictions, and our pain. Gentle and loving Spirit/God, shelter us in the fold of your arms. Let nothing either distress or disturb our hearts. Reveal to us your grace, so that we may find our miracle and the miracle of the world. Most Holy Spirit/God, make us messengers of your will. Amen."

Afterword

The Gift of Happily Ever After
I had the opportunity to fly up to New York for a couple of days. This would be my second visit to St. Patrick's Cathedral. I was very excited to go back, after feeling such grace and peace with my first visit in March 2006, when I had lit three candles.

I was planning on spending the morning of my last New York day there. I embarked from my hotel and hopped in a cab. I excitedly told the cab driver, "St. Patrick's Cathedral, please." The cab pulled down a side street and dropped me off in front of the side entrance steps to the church. I stepped out of the cab and before I had two feet on the ground, I heard, "Good morning, princess!"

I thought to myself, *Okay, did I just hear someone say that?* I closed the cab door and proceeded up the steps of the church's side entrance. Each step up somehow felt closer and closer to an amazing calm. The voice I'd heard was coming from an older gentleman of Spanish descent who was a church attendant/security guard standing at the top of the stairs . . . and, yes, he was talking to me. As he opened the door for me, he again said to me very slowly, looking right in my eyes, "Hello, beautiful princess."

I was a little taken aback by the fact that I was there to light a candle for my mother for the very first time following her death in September, and how she had called me a beautiful princess when I was a little girl.

I walked through the door, and the attendant followed me in. He said, "My name is Freddie, and if you need me, I will be here." I found this funny because my mother would always tell me make-believe stories and would often name the male characters "Freddie." I thanked Freddie and introduced myself, as well.

I continued into the church and went off to the left, up to the very front near the altar. St. Patrick's Cathedral is such a marvelous and sacred structure . . . so captivating and magnificent. I did a complete circle of the church, because I wanted to find the perfect altar spot to light my four candles and sit for the morning. St. Patrick's is such a huge church and there are many beautiful places to choose from.

I came to the perfect spot. There wasn't a doubt in my mind that this is where I would light the candles. I picked an altar with a big beautiful oil painting of the Lady of Guadelupe, which was hung from the ceiling. There were many bouquets of fresh flowers all around it, and it was the only altar in the church with *real* flowers. The setting was beautiful, and made me feel so peaceful and special.

For the first time ever, I lit the four candles to represent my mother, father, and two brothers. As I lit them, I stepped back; and as I looked at those four candles, I was surprisingly overwhelmed and saddened—I had a massive amount of grief. Tears fell, and I turned away to quickly find a seat. I could barely see because of my tears, and had to lean and grab the back of the first pew to hold myself up. Then I slowly sat down in the second pew. I totally wasn't expecting this outpouring of emotion.

Tears kept falling as I looked at my candles—tears not only of sadness, but also of complete peace. I asked someone for a tissue, but came up empty. A few moments later, Freddie appeared with two big napkins. He handed them over and said in his Spanish accent, "This is actually my area that I am in charge of. Let me do something special for you."

He walked over to the same candles, lit two, bowed his head, and said a prayer. He turned back to me and said, "Don't cry, don't cry, you'll be okay. You will go *home* today and you'll be okay."

How did he know I was going home today? I thought. All I could get out was, "Thank you," and then more tears came. I tried to gather my composure and sat still in my pew for a few moments to journal my feelings. Just being there, I enjoyed the presence of the cathedral. I continued to cry off and on as I was journaling, and I prayed for a long while. I was just so sad.

Then, about a half hour later, I heard my name called out loud: "Tina!" I looked up and Freddie was standing behind the candles up in the altar, right next to the Lady of Guadalupe painting. He pointed to one white rose among all the flowers, and pulled it out of the vase, holding it up—showing me that it was for me. He turned back to the painting while holding the beautiful, long-stemmed rose and said another prayer.

He then came out from behind the altar and walked this beautiful long-stemmed white rose to me. It was the same as the white rose I had picked from my mother's casket the day of her burial. I knew instantly that it was from my mother. As he handed me the rose, he said, "Here:

this is for you." I immediately started to weep. What an amazing gift from Spirit. He then sat down beside me, pointed back up to the Lady of Guadalupe, and very softly whispered to me, "Mommy told me to do that, and I always listen to her."

I am truly and deeply amazed at the awesome presence of Spirit. I feel there is yet a lot to unfold, but I have become a receptacle and the "seed" of clear sight and creativity has been planted within.

Reach for clarity, follow an illumined path, and pursue the happiness your soul desires. The pursuit of happiness is a journey of empowerment and wholeness. Peace on earth starts right here and right now, with you. Discovering and living your own personal happiness, wholeness, and peace is *your* gift to impart to the world.

By using these gifts and the Gift of Spirit, you are simultaneously regifting to the world. It is a win-win gift to the world. I love these gifts. I love *love*. I love believing, enchantment, "fairy dust," rainbows, and butterflies. I love everything light and magical. This, to me, is heaven on earth. I love God and Spirit for where I am today; for with them, anything is possible—anything.

I sit here today in front of a beautiful harbor in Florida, writing this final chapter. Above me is a clear blue sky. Before me is the twinkling of the bright sunlight along the water. And out on the water are four sailboats anchored just beyond the markers, all facing north. These four boats tell me that, today, there is only one way to go, one direction to follow. To deny this truth would be to deny my soul's light and *your* soul's light. To deny this truth would only lead to prolonged suffering and darkness. And life was not meant to be lived in suffering; rather, it was meant to be lived in bliss, peace, and abundance.

My wish for you is that, wherever you are on your spiritual journey, you have found in these pages (and will continue to find) the spirit of healing, understanding, and self-enlightenment. For that is what our souls most desire in this lifetime. Rise above and you will continue to see the grace of God and the messages from Spirit.

I hope you feel my presence come through the pages with my arms open to embrace you, as a light, as a comfort, and as a friend. Writing this book has been a wondrous journey. Every moment was a precious unveiling of words. It has felt from the beginning—when it was just a seed—that with Spirit and the opening of my heart and soul, with my vulnerability and love, and with your open-mindedness and willingness to look deeper and further, eventually the spring would come and the seed would become a magnificent rose.

I have found solace and comfort, delight and wisdom come to me through the writing of this book, which has miraculously benefited the development of who I am and the empowerment of my own soul. I sincerely wish the same for you. I have experienced firsthand the indomitable will of the Universe; and now these chapters, these gifts, I pass to you—it is in your precious hands. Step forward confidently and with faith, placing your pen to page . . . the rest of your life is unwritten.

May your "fairy tale" unfold and your life become enchanted. May you be blessed with joy, sacred love, higher consciousness, peace, health, healing, light, and prosperity.

As I end this book with these final sentences, I hear the words from within my heart, and I bow to you to say *Peace be with you*. And I hear you reply, *And also with you*. Blessed be.

And we all lived happily ever after.

☞ Appendix ☜

More on Feng Shui

If you would like to go into further depth about the philosophy and practice of feng shui, you can use this appendix to study and reference, according to your desire. Hopefully, you'll be inspired to further explore this ancient, rich, rewarding field and use it to enhance many aspects of your life.

Feng Shui Curative Elements/Enhancements

In feng shui, you can use a variety of curative elements and enhancements to start changing the energy in your environment for the better. Here is a basic list:

> *Colors*—Feng shui has a lot to say about colors. Every color holds a unique vibration and special meaning. From our bedding, towels, furniture, carpet, nail polish, and clothing, to the exterior wall paint applied to our home, we implement color into every fiber of our surroundings.

Statues/rocks—These represent stability and grounding and provide a sense of security. Using solid objects implements a grounding energy, thus having a stabilizing effect.

Wind chimes/flags—These call in and attract positive energy. The wind carries an intrinsic energy that can call in and cultivate positive forces, in terms of the feng shui of your space. Just think of when you are riding in a convertible or standing on the shoreline; you can feel the wind's energetic affect.

Crystals—Crystals attract and keep the good chi flowing. When used correctly, crystals can oppress negative energy. Also, through the simple properties that crystals hold, a rainbow spectrum is naturally generated that can attract, reflect, and continually radiate good energy (similar to rainbows in the sky).

Plants/flowers/trees—Whether real or artificial, these represent growth and nurturing. Plants, flowers, and trees are elements of the earth, conveying the beneficial effects that nature has on one's surroundings, including the beauty that affects your chi and well-being in auspicious ways.

Mirrors—Mirrors are powerful transformers of energy, based on the principle that mirrors can transcendentally move the energy in one's realm. Mirrors are considered the "miracle pill in feng shui," because they're the most widely used of all the cures. Mirrors can set forth double the energy they are reflecting, thus facilitating doubly good chi flow. Mirrors can also deflect negative energy.

By using one or a combination of these feng shui curative elements and enhancements, a feng shui consultant can help any person's home have a more positive energetic flow and a greater feeling of harmony throughout it.

There are many different styles of feng shui; the main influence on my training and background has been the Black Sect Style, under Master Lin Yun, but I have also studied Compass Style. Today, the Black Sect Style is the most popular form of feng shui in the United States.

The Bagua

The Bagua is a tool that is composed of the concept of yin/yang; the five elements (wood, wind, fire, earth, and metal); associations; and the *I Ching,* an ancient text of Oriental philosophy, the title of which translates to *The Chinese Book of Changes.* Using the Bagua map shown here, I will address each of the nine stations, representing nine major areas of life: Knowledge, Career, Benefactors (Helpful People), Family, Health, Children, Wealth, Fame, and Marriage (Relationships).

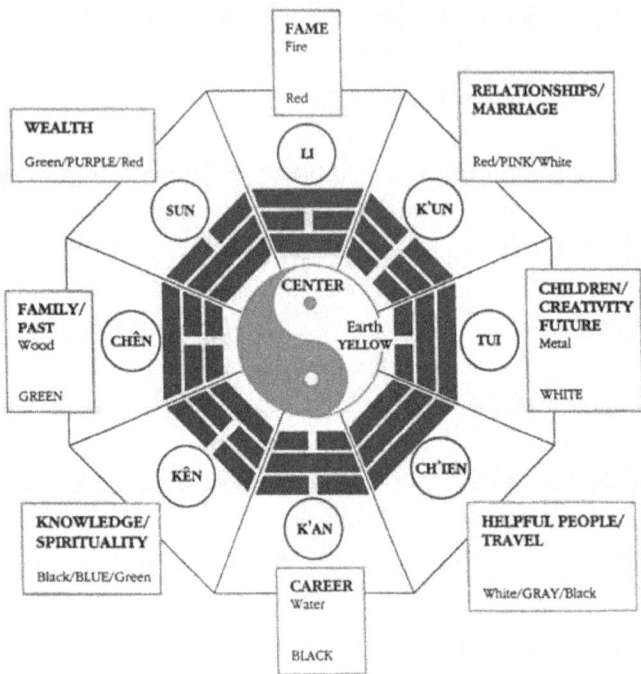

FAME
Fire

Red

RELATIONSHIPS/
MARRIAGE

WEALTH

Green/PURPLE/Red

Red/PINK/White

LI

SUN

K'UN

CENTER

CHILDREN/
CREATIVITY
FUTURE
Metal

FAMILY/
PAST
Wood

Earth
YELLOW

CHÊN

TUI

GREEN

WHITE

KÊN

CH'IEN

KNOWLEDGE/
SPIRITUALITY

K'AN

HELPFUL PEOPLE/
TRAVEL

Black/BLUE/Green

CAREER
Water

White/GRAY/Black

BLACK

The Bagua

The Bagua is easier to understand if you do a diagram on tracing paper of a tic-tac-toe template. This, too, will represent the nine stations, as shown in the diagram below. When placing this map over the layout of your home, a particular room, a desk, or lot of land, the bottom row is always the location of the entrance. Therefore, your entrance is always in one of the following three bottom-row stations: Knowledge (also known as Wisdom of Spirituality), Career, or Helpful People/ Travel (also known as Guardian Angel and Benefactors). For instance, if your front door is positioned on the right as you face the entrance, it is in the Helpful People, or *ch'ien,* area.

Wealth	Fame	Marriage
Family	Health	Children
Knowledge	Career	Helpful People

-- -- -- E n t r a n c e -- -- --

Kên: Knowledge

The lower left-hand corner/section of your home, when facing the entrance, is the *kên* section, or the Knowledge/ Wisdom section. Spirituality, contemplation and cultivation are also included in this area. The association for this section is Mountain. The color commonly associated with this section is blue. Black and green are also commonly associated with this area. Plants, flowers, and stones/crystals, which represent the earth element (mountains come from the earth) produce a favorable energy and represent clear-headedness, increasing wisdom and understanding. Placing these items in your Knowledge and Wisdom section and setting your intentions as to the kind of knowledge you would like to cultivate can help change the energy for the better.

Kên: Knowledge		

A perfect example of the Knowledge section can be found in many homes across America. Often garages exist in this Knowledge and Wisdom section of one's house. A typical Florida-home resident, for example, called me for a consult. She was working from home, and thought it would be valuable for her to get the energy flowing correctly in her home so that she could be more successful. However, her entire garage was located in the Knowledge and Wisdom section.

She had four children and the garage was a complete mess, with bikes, scooters, and sports equipment scattered everywhere. After taking a look at the garage, I said to her, "You probably are feeling like you can't think straight or stay focused with whatever task you have at hand. And you probably feel confused and lack clarity about your home business *and* your personal life."

She heartily agreed and said that this clutter, confusion, and lack of clarity were the reasons for calling me to her home. I explained to her the importance of keeping the Knowledge area, her garage, clean and organized. If not, I warned her, it will be a continuing struggle to focus, meditate, nurture her children, and increase her own wisdom and understanding. The following weekend, she cleared out the entire garage and made rules for the children to do their part in maintaining the garage's orderliness. She called me months later to report that her home life and home business were running like a well-oiled machine.

Here are some feng shui tips for this section:

Making sure the Knowledge/Wisdom section of your home is clean and clutter-free leads to optimal learning, so this is particularly important if you have children. (It is also important that a child's room be clean and uncluttered.)

The Knowledge/Wisdom area is a great place to put a desk or bookshelf. Additionally, having an office in this area is very conducive to knowledge and wisdom for the occupants and for a successful business.

K'an: Career

The lower middle section of your home, when facing the entrance is the *k'an* section, or the Career section. The element for this section is water. The associated color for this section is black. Water elements such as fountains, pictures of water, and anything that is black or has black in it are very propitious and represents growth and nurturing of your career. Placing these items in your Career section and setting your intention for your career are valuable ways to change the energy for the better.

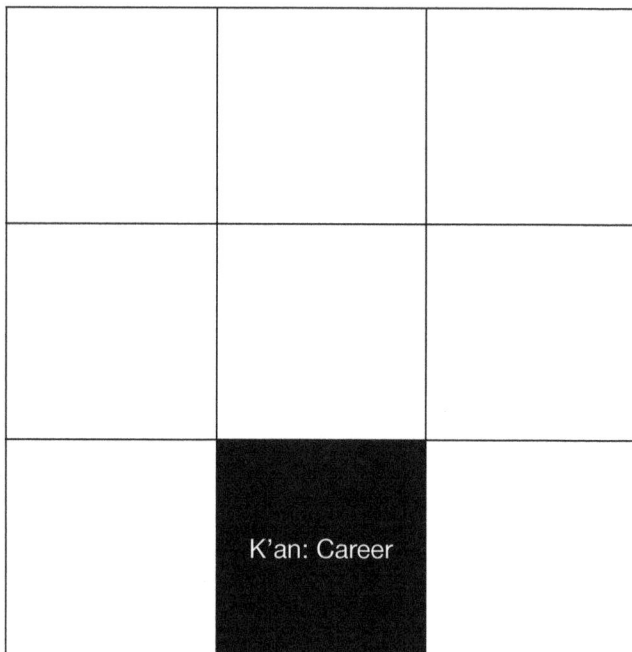

	K'an: Career	

When placing a water element in your home, make sure the water flows *toward* the home and not away from it. I once did a consultation for a New Age store that had in its entryway a beautiful lotus waterfall . . . and the flow of water was directed right back out the door. So, I pointed out to the owner that the positive energy coming from this beautiful waterfall was leaving the store every time a customer walked in! I suggested we move the waterfall toward the front door, facing in. As a result of the feng shui enhancements and my recommendations, this store outgrew itself within three months. It ended up undergoing a huge expansion and eventually grew into a complete wellness center, which was the owner's ultimate dream. This is a perfect example of business owners setting an intention for their careers and following their dreams.

Another business consult I did was for a wellness clinic in St. Augustine, Florida, that specialized in colonics. The owner was very eager to hear all of the suggestions to improve the energy of her clinic and implemented the changes immediately. Here is what she wrote to me:

> My most sincere appreciation to you, Tina, for your talent and spirit. The feng shui assessment you did for my clinic was not only fascinating, but also very effective. You really took the time to explain the *wheres* and *whys* of our energy and vibrations. We made the modifications to our establishment that you recommended and we are having a record year!

Here are a few more feng shui tips for this section:

If applicable, write on your business card specifically what it is you wish to become or what you wish to make from your career. Place the card in the front middle section of your desk or desk drawer.

Incorporate something black in the career section of your home. For example, choose something solid, like a heavy black object, to represent strength, or black-framed pictures that can represent structure.

This section has everything to do with new beginnings and opportunities; so make sure this area in your home is open and receptive to receive those things.

Ch'ien: Helpful People • Travel

The near right-hand corner/section of your home, when facing the entrance, is the *ch'ien* section: the Helpful People and Travel section. Guardian angels and benefactors are also included in this section. The elemental association for this section is heaven. The colors associated with this section are gray and silver. Plants, flowers, stones/crystals, and anything that specifically represents the heaven element to you are very auspicious. Placing these items in your Guardian Angel, Helpful People, and Travel section and setting your intention for what guardian angels and what helpful people you want in your life and what kind of traveling you want to do can improve the energy in your home or office, and make a dramatic improvement in the quality of your life.

		Ch'ien: Helpful People, Travel

Helpful people can be your business clients or the people you encounter every day, as well as your family and friends who help and support you. From your hair dresser to the lawn man, from your mortgage broker to your accountant, from your employer or employee to the Starbucks girl who makes you the perfect skinny vanilla latte—anyone who potentially can help your life is included under "helpful people." Travel is also in this section and stands for safe, abundant, and enriching travel. Guardian angels offer healing, protection, support, and love.

Here are your feng shui tips for this section:

If you have a front-door entrance that is in the ch'ien section, you can enhance it by placing a pair of fu dogs or lions for protection. Fu dogs offer protection from evil, sickness, and bad chi from entering your domain. Lions also offer protection. Lion energy placed at the front entrance is protective, powerful, and majestic. This provides great and clear energy coming into the entrance of your home.

A mirror placed anywhere around the outer front door or door frame, facing out—to reflect negative or sick energy from your home—is also auspicious. Serious feng shui-ists will have a Bagua mirror above their front doors. But anything reflective, even a window in your door or a shiny front door, will do fine.

Any flags, statues, or crystals in the ch'ien area of your home will call in helpful-people energy. Placing an angel, "fairy dust" (glitter or crystallized powder/sparkles), or something from a deceased love one—such as a picture, holy card, anything of remembrance—will call in Spirit energy, guardian-angel energy, and healing and protection energy. Remember: it's about whatever you feel should be in this space that's congruent with your beliefs, religion, and intuition.

Chên: Family

The middle left-hand section of your home, when facing the entrance, is the *chên* section, or the Family section. The color for this section is green. The element is wood. Enhancements to place in this section are vibrant indoor trees and plants, either live or silk, anything with the color green or made of wood, and anything that symbolizes or represents something meaningful to you about your family. Placing these items in your Family section and setting your intentions for your family will improve the likelihood of the energy in your home or office changing for the better.

Chên: Family		

The Family section directly relates to both your immediate family *and* your extended family: your mother, father, brothers, aunts, uncles, cousins, etc. Is there harmony, unity, and peace in your family? Take a look at what is in the Family section of your home, and then take a look at what is going on in your family dynamics. Make sure that this area is free from clutter and disorganization.

The kitchen in my current home is located partly in the family section, and I enhanced this section by painting the inside walls of my pantry in a Ralph Lauren shade called Kauai. It is a light and peaceful green. And we all want our family to be light and peaceful, don't we?

In my last home, I did the same thing but chose a color called Kamaka Island (a teal green/blue hue). It was a very "islandy" and "cool" color. And this reflected in the extended family being very "cool" and laid back.

Here are a couple of feng shui tips for this section:

Photos of your family are best kept in this section. A great time for changes and enhancements for the family section and setting your intention is during your preparation for the holidays. Need I say more?

The element for the family section is wood; so photo frames made out of wood, hardwood floors, and wooden furniture are all beneficial in this area, enhancing the overall chi and contributing in positive ways to your relationships with your family.

Health (Center of Bagua)

The middle section of your home, when facing the entrance, ties into the *kun* section and is the Health and Unity section. The element for this section is earth. The colors for this section are yellow and gold hues. Plants, flowers, and stones/crystals, which represent the earth element, are very auspicious and are tied to wholeness and health energy. Placing these items in your Health section and setting your intention for your physical, emotional, and mental health will assist in changing the energy for the better.

	Health	

Here are your feng shui tips for this section:

My favorite enhancement for this area is to have an aurora borealis crystal hung with golden or yellow ribbon nine inches from the ceiling. (The number nine is auspicious in feng shui because it signifies completion, accomplishment, and attainment) High-quality crystals with an aurora borealis finish reflect all the colors of the rainbow and the Bagua. As you hang your crystal, you set your intention and prayer for health and wellness for yourself and for the rest of the occupants in your home.

A very important thing to consider is the quality of the air you breathe in your home. This can dramatically improve not only your health, but also the energy of your home. Poor air quality, dust, mites, and mold all result in sickness. We've all heard of sick-building syndrome or how easy it can be for mold to grow inside the walls of your home. Really take a deep breath when standing in the center of your home. Using your intuition and body, you can make an assessment of the air quality of your home. Air purifiers are an added benefit and very much worth the cost, in my opinion. Salt-rock lamps have great effects on the air, too. Salt rock is similar to an ionizer, in that it permeates the air with negative ions, which are believed to purify the air and kill bacteria, thereby helping to relieve sinus problems, allergies, and colds. It also can help with anxiety, insomnia, and even psoriasis and emphysema.

Tui: Creativity • Children

The middle/right section of your home, when facing the entrance, is the *tui* section, or the Creativity and Children section. The element for this section is metal. The color for this section is white. Plants, flowers, stones/crystals, and anything white and/or metal are all propitious and represent your creativity and your children. Placing these items in your Creativity and Children section and setting your intention for expressing your creativity in your life and nurturing your children (if any) will ensure that the energy will likely change for the better.

		Tui: Creativity, Children

A client had her laundry room in the Creativity and Children section, which was piled high with laundry, disorganized, and not decorated at all. She told me she had felt unclear about what her purpose in life was and felt overwhelmed by the day-to-day routine and needs of her two children.

I explained to her that her Creativity and Children section was in the laundry room. I suggested she start by decorating the area. She found and hung a cute old-fashioned sign over the door of the laundry room that said "Wash Room" with a picture of a washing bucket from the "olden days." By luck, her washer and dryer were white and, of course, metal, which is both the correct color and the correct element for this section. So, by keeping this area clean and the dirty clothes, laundry supplies, iron/ironing board, and all other related items organized, the energy would quickly begin to flow correctly and positively.

I also asked her to set her intentions in regard to her creativity and her children, and to earnestly reflect about her own personal needs, since I saw that she could truly use a space for her creativity to be nourished and grow. The intentions behind her enhancing her laundry room set forth a positive energy in her and in her home, which helped her become more clear, and eventually changed her feelings of being overwhelmed with her children or burdened by the chores she faced daily.

Here are two feng shui tips for this section:

On the laundry-room note, I would like to say this is where I recommend keeping all dirty laundry. Dirty laundry and dirty laundry baskets should be kept *out* of all bathrooms and definitely out of all bedrooms.

Using the element of metal and the color white are very positive contributions to one's creative emergence. Placing these objects can counter stagnant thinking or low creativity.

Sun: Wealth

The upper left-hand corner/section of your home, when facing the entrance, is the *sun* section, or the Wealth section. Wealth in feng shui is beyond the monetary. So many of us feel that money is the most important thing in our lives. Feng shui views wealth as fortunate blessings and abundance on all levels of your life: mental, emotional, physical and spiritual.

The element for this section is wind. The main color for this section is purple, although red and green are also auspicious to use here. Plants, flowers, stones/crystals, and anything colored purple conveys favorable energy and represent growth, abundance, and fortunate blessings. Placing these items in your Wealth section and setting your intention for having, enjoying, and sharing abundant wealth will support a positive change in the energy of your home and/or office.

Sun: Wealth		

I was called to be part of the planning and construction process of a new home in a prestigious community in West Palm Beach, Florida. I would be implementing feng shui principles and giving the overall approval for the layout of both the home and the landscaping. The family wanted a beautiful large pool and wanted to add rocks and waterfall elements. They were amazed to learn my reasoning for the placement of the pool, and were very pleased with where I actually placed the pool and how the whole pool enhances the home, both aesthetically and energetically.

I placed the pool in the Wealth section of the lot so the water in that section would bring in abundance and an *ocean* of prosperity. I also worked with the pool designer to set the pool in a natural curved shape so that it hugged the home, as if in an embrace. This, I explained, would hold prosperity *in* while continuing to draw in good wealth. The rocks that made a huge waterfall (the highest aspect of the pool itself) were designed to go in the uppermost corner and come down toward the home. This gave it a complete look of an oasis and a feeling of having this huge, solid structure—gushing and trickling water coming down toward the home, generating energy and wealth into the home and the lives of the occupants. We used palm trees and other plants to represent growth and abundance.

Here are a few feng shui tips for this section:

Clear out clutter! Having clutter in the Wealth area can create financial problems in your life. And *lots* of clutter can be financially devastating! Having a feng shui cure (a mirror, for example) in this area to generate more wealth will actually cause *double* financial hardship if the area is cluttered. Clear out your clutter so that you can welcome and make room for new abundance! Use feng shui cures such as mirrors, lively plants, colors, and crystals to call in wealth energy.

Since the element for prosperity is wind, wind chimes are very auspicious to place in this section.

A small mound of gold nuggets (if necessary, you can use gold spray paint on small rocks or pebbles) placed in the garden or by the front door, and/or gold lights on any indoor or outdoor trees (including a Christmas tree, if you put one up), will assist in bringing in prosperity, luck, and good fortune! Luminous golden light indicates the power of the mind and creativity, which may encourage you and give you a sense of marked clarity, thereby inspiring you to create new resolutions in your life. The brown trunk of the tree represents grounding energy, and should be meditated on. It also represents our spine, which holds us upright, acting as a channel for our energy and enabling us to carry the weight of our lives.

Be happy for and hold a positive attitude toward others' good fortune! Bless another's good fortune by thinking kind thoughts toward others' wealth, and know there is plenty for all of us! When you celebrate and think kind thoughts toward another's fortune, you rejuvenate your own calling and energetically open your own gateway of fortune and abundance.

Li: Fame

The upper-middle section of your home, when facing the entrance, is the *li* section, or the Fame section (also known as Illumination). The element for this section is fire. The colors for this section are red and orange. Plants, trees, wood, and anything red or orange (which either represents fire or feeds fire) are quite auspicious and represent the good characteristics of having fame. Fame or illumination refers to one's image or standing in the community—your reputation. Placing the aforementioned items in your Fame section and setting your intention on having a positive, spiritually integral quality of fame about you will contribute to an improved, uplifted energy in your home and/or work environment.

	Li: Fame	

One day, a newscaster came to my home to do an interview segment on feng shui. The newscaster, Lisa, had just moved down south from up north, and had just landed this position as a newscaster with a local ABC network. After the videotaping was completed, we sat talking about her recent move, her new job, and how feng shui would make a difference in her transition to the area. I talked to her about concentrating her focus on the Fame section of her new apartment, as it would represent how she would develop professionally and come to be known (i.e., her professional reputation).

I asked Lisa to make a list of her intentions, how she wanted her viewers to accept and think of her, and how she wanted coworkers and the head production staff to view her. I then told her to decorate her Fame area to match her passion and desires. Five years later, she is going strong, having received a recent promotion and a very positive viewer response.

Here are your feng shui tips for this section:

This area should represent your passions and should serve as inspiration to you. Place in this area artwork, curtains, furniture, or anything else that reflects your feelings of passion and inspiration.

Place red or wooden items in this area to represent fire and passion (wood feeds fire).

Do not have any water in this area, as water puts out fire. If you have a pool in the Fame area of your lot, place red or terra cotta pots of flowers or trees around the perimeter of the pool, or make sure that the pavers around the pool are a reddish color (this will balance the fire/water energy set forth by the pool).

On a spiritual level, Fame (and illumination) concerns self-realization and enlightenment. In 2000 I had my favorite photographer come over to my home to take a Christmas portrait and a picture for the family's Christmas cards. She took one picture of me by myself, nestled on a chair, with amazing light coming in, while I was reading a book. It came out beautifully, and she recommended using it as a portrait. For over a decade now, I've had it hanging on the highest floor in my home, in the Fame section. It wasn't until I sat down to put this book together a few years ago that the portrait resonated a total connection with me, giving me a sort of spiritual realization. This portrait is of me with my book, and this book is what I want most to be known for.

Kun: Marriage

The upper right-hand corner/section of your home, when facing the entrance, is the *kun* section, or the Marriage section. Partnership and motherhood are also considered part of this section. I like to call it the Love section. The element for this section is earth. The colors for this section are pink, red, and peach. Plants, flowers, and stones/crystals, which represent the earth element, are favorable to the increase of positive energy and represent growth and nurturing of your current partnerships. Placing these items in your Love, Marriage/Partnership, and Motherhood section and setting your intention for your primary relationships can greatly enhance the energy in your home and/or office.

		Kun: Marriage

I was doing a television segment on the local Fox morning show. It was an all-morning event that followed me throughout the morning "feng shui-ing" of a new client's home. The reporter was Russell Rhodes; and though we hadn't previously met each other, we instantly hit it off. He understood a little about feng shui, but was very interested to learn more and seemed excited to participate in the process. Between the commercials and other breaks, we spent time talking. I was fueling his brain with tidbits of feng shui knowledge, which he seemed to be soaking up like a sponge. He had a happy, positive disposition and was so joyfully eager to learn more.

So, Russell was standing there, saying, "Tell me more, tell me more." Trying to come up with something quick that we hadn't already addressed, I said, "Your handsome shirt—your shirt is pink, and I can tell by not only the color but also by your energy wearing the shirt that you are opening your heart chakra to love. Wearing that shirt today denotes a readiness to wear your heart on your sleeve. You're ready, aren't you?"

He was shocked and found this amazing. He said he really felt like wearing that shirt today, and while dressing that morning and on the drive over, he was thinking about being single, and that he might be ready to open himself up and start dating.

Here are some feng shui tips for this section:

Candles in feng shui offer soft yin (feminine) energy and are great to have in in your Love, Marriage/Partnership, and Motherhood section. Ideally, use white for purity, peach, red, or pink.

Keep your master bedroom free from clutter. Clutter in your bedroom will clutter your relationship. Make your bedroom a space to nurture yourself and your partner.

Make changes so that your bedroom becomes a "love palace" or "hotel suite." Try adding different touches, such as luxurious, high-quality bedding, a minifridge, chandeliers, floral arrangements, beautiful art, etc.

As for underneath the bed, recognize that everything in your energy space affects the quality of your sleep. Therefore, clear under your bed and give the floor a nice vacuum. I love vacuuming; it automatically lifts the energy and feels so good.

If you've had your mattress in previous relationships, toss it and buy a new mattress. It will subconsciously affect you. I call it "bed karma." (My twist on "bad karma") At the least, you should sage the mattress (by burning sage over and around it) or energetically clear the space (and the mattress) by sprinkling it with holy water (or something else that has a cleansing meaning to you). Doing either of these suggestions will clear and cleanse the energy. Then put on a new mattress cover or a new feather bed on top, along with new sheets. The intention is to alleviate the past, cleaning our slate, so as to nurture and revere the beginning of a new love.

If you can see the toilet from where you lay your head down in bed, make sure you keep the toilet lid down and the bathroom door closed. Open toilets carry a negative chi and can pull down and "flush" good energy.

Feng Shui Enhancements: Finding Love

My favorite feng shui enhancement for finding a partner to share your love with is to light a candle; either a pink (the color representing love and partnership) or a vanilla (the scent of vanilla opens one's heart chakra) is great. Place the candle on the upper-right hand corner of your nightstand, which is the love/partnership section. Then write a letter or a card and keep it by the candle. The letter can be a journaling, or maybe a letter to God or a letter to the person you would like to call in. Describe the qualities you are looking for, and what kind of love you want to manifest. Explain what you have gone through, where you are at this moment in time, what you've learned, and what you would like to accomplish together. Keep this letter by the candle or away in a designated special place. Light the candle any time you feel compelled to, and let it burn for any length of time you feel compelled to. Remember to use your intuition to personalize this enhancement. When it comes to feng shui, you must learn to trust yourself and what feels right to you. This enhancement not only sorts out and brings forward your inner feelings, but it also sets forth to Spirit your intention of finding love.

Be creative when doing feng shui, and always use your own intuition. If compelled to do so, light a candle at a special time every night, or pray, or repeat some affirmations aloud. All of this will invoke positive energy. And this positive energy sets up manifestation. One of my favorite love enhancements is to write down positive affirmations that pertain to your love and relationship desires. Keep them by your bedside. Say and think about them each morning upon arising, in order to open up the gates of manifestation. Don't worry about how on earth they will happen; just allow them to become part of your conscious mind as intention and prayer.

Partnership Feng Shui and Scent

The sense of smell can powerfully affect the mind and body. By appealing to the sense of smell, we can communicate on an instinctive level to open and attract partnerships. Through the dimension of scent you can attune yourself to the vibration of love.

Vanilla, patchouli, bergamot, and lavender are favorite scents for men. Men are attracted to these. These ingredients are often used in colognes, candles, bath products, and essential oils. A lot of times, colognes carry earthy tones that make a man smell masculine and woodsy, and then there are elements that represent being free-spirited. Coriander seed is really unusual, and is sometimes used in "love potions" to act on the heart chakra, and thus is suitable for a period of engagement and weddings, especially when the bond is intended to last beyond space and time. Clary sage is another unusual fragrance, one that helps one release tension and gain spiritual perspective and understanding, and assists in purification and protection.

For women, smelling notes of grapefruit will assist with self-confidence, clearing negative emotions from past relationships, and overcoming jealousy, bitterness, and frustration. The scent of ylang-ylang is used to attract love, enhance sensuality, and assist one in letting go of guilt and anger. And fragrance notes of rose are used for love, happiness, peace, and compassion. The fragrance of rose also opens the heart chakra while dispelling fears and sadness. The scent of patchouli has been known to be a potent aphrodisiac, and that of neroli is used to open one's heart chakra, clear mental confusion, and attract positive energy and happiness! You can use an essential oil alone or research the notes of any specific perfume. Vanilla notes are my personal favorite, since they can open your heart chakra, denoting an open heart and a readiness to wear your heart on your sleeve. Vanilla also has properties that stimulate one's energy and mental powers.

My Feng Shui Favorites

Painting a feature wall in your home in a strong color is excellent feng shui. Choose a wall in the living or dining room. It doesn't always have to be "feng shui red." A golden- or yellow-toned wall can stand for health, love, romance, and strong, healthy relationships. The important thing is to use the Bagua color guide and your intuition, feeling for yourself what specific colors you're drawn toward, especially in deciding your wall colors and accent colors. It can vary from room to room or you may have a very strong feeling to have the whole house in the same soft color, (which I've always been inclined to do) and use stronger colors in your fabrics and furnishings.

There are in-style colors and themes for every season, but my favorite is fall/winter. You can just take a look at any Pottery Barn holiday issue, or any other catalogs, for ideas about what resonates with you. These colors and themes are also splashed throughout department stores. Getting to know what colors you're drawn to is an excellent way to incorporate feng shui savvy into your life. For example, imagine a color palette of dark brown and blue with hints of gray. In feng shui, brown stands for stability, grounding, and long-established enduring qualities and elegance. Pale blue represents heavenly peace, hope, and new beginnings. One of my personal favorites—I absolutely love this—is pale blue painted on the ceilings of a home or office to symbolize heavenly peace and the ascent of prayer. Gray can be incorporated for peace and harmony, and for resolving conflicts in the home, which is perfectly appropriate for not only the holiday season, but also all year round!

About the Author

Tina Coluccio is a renowned spiritual intuitive and practicing Feng Shui consultant, with a background in the medical field as a nurse. Ms. Coluccio has done hundreds of in-home and business Feng Shui consultations, as well as innumerable personal spiritual consultations.

Ms. Coluccio lectures extensively on a variety of esoteric subjects, including energy healing and Feng Shui, and has appeared often in both print and television media.

Continually updating and expanding her knowledge of Feng Shui, while availing herself to all who seek "spirit guidance," Tina has remained dedicated to helping others find their sacred balance and spiritual well-being.

www.ingramcontent.com/pod-product-compliance
Lightning Source LLC
Chambersburg PA
CBHW032058080426
42733CB00006B/331